D1255350

ANSWERS TO GOSPEL QUESTIONS

Answers to Gospel Questions

Joseph Fielding Smith

Volume IV

Published by

Deseret Book Company
44 East South Temple
Salt Lake City, Utah

SECOND PRINTING

Printed by

DESERET NEWS PRESS

in the United States of America

FOREWORD

The Apostle Peter wrote in his first general epistle to the Saints in the Meridian of Time, "But sanctify the Lord God in your hearts: and be ready always to give an answer to every man that asketh you a reason of the hope that is in you with meekness and fear."[1]

The Apostle Paul gave similar advice in his epistle to the Colossian Saints wherein he wrote: "Let your speech be alway with grace, seasoned with salt, that ye may know how ye ought to answer every man."[2]

As members of The Church of Jesus Christ of Latter-day Saints the Lord has admonished us to gain knowledge and understanding of gospel principles that we, too, may "be ready always to give an answer to every man" for our faith in the restored gospel. We have been commanded to "seek learning, even by study and also by faith."[3]

No other organization on the face of this earth has offered so much opportunity to gain knowledge of God and his gospel as has The Church of Jesus Christ of Latter-day Saints. Inspired prophets, revelation, the standard works, and also priesthood and auxiliary organizations for all ages have afforded us opportunity to learn all that God has revealed.

Through years of experience, President Joseph Fielding Smith is one of those who has benefited from these sources of knowledge and prepared himself to

---

[1] I Peter 3:15.
[2] Colossians 4:6.
[3] D. & C. 88:118.

give ready answers to every man. From his own testimony the following is quoted:

"Among these things I remember that one thing I did from the time I learned to read and write was to study the gospel. I read and committed to memory the children's catechism and primary books on the gospel. Later I read the History of the Church as recorded in the *Millennial Star*. I also read the Bible, the Book of Mormon, Pearl of Great Price, and the Doctrine and Covenants, and other literature which fell into my hands. . . . I learned at a very early day that God lives; he gave me a testimony when I was a child, and I have tried to be obedient always with some measure of success."[4]

Calling upon President Smith's vast knowledge and experience, this fourth volume of *Answers to Gospel Questions* has been prepared and published with a desire that others may enhance their knowledge through a careful study of questions and answers contained therein.

Appreciation is expressed to *The Improvement Era* for permission to use articles that have appeared in their regular monthly feature entitled, "Your Question." Additional answers to questions have been added by President Smith for publication in this volume.

—JOSEPH FIELDING SMITH, JR.

---

[4]Excerpt from letter to Joseph Fielding Smith, Jr. while serving as a missionary in Great Britain.

CONTENTS

PAGE

INTRODUCTION

Behold, I stand at the door, and knock: if any man hear my voice, and open the door, I will come in to him, and will sup with him, and he with me.

To him that overcometh will I grant to sit with me in my throne, even as I also overcame, and am set down with my Father in his throne.[1]

Each member of the Church was blessed and received the gift of the Holy Ghost after baptism. It seems, however, that there are some among us who expect the Lord to enlighten their minds and give them knowledge without their putting forth any effort by study and by faith. They evidently received a testimony after they were confirmed, but from that time forth they never did any thing to keep that testimony alive. Therefore they have ceased to grow spiritually and the light which was first given has become dimmed through their inactivity.

We have been warned by the prophets of old and also by the Son of God that the Spirit will not always strive with men. Unless we exercise faith and seek through prayer and study to know the truth and to walk in spiritual light, the inspiration that once was ours becomes dimmed and may go out altogether. If we thus permit the light we once received to die then we are likely to become a prey to the sorcerer and the cunning deceiver. When this condition prevails the time may come when the person forgets that he ever had the light. Peter has expressed this condition in forceful language as follows:

For if after they have escaped the pollutions of the world through the knowledge of the Lord and Saviour Jesus Christ, they are again entangled therein, and overcome, the latter end is worse with them than the beginning.

For it had been better for them not to have known the way

---

[1]Revelation 3:20-21.

of righteousness, than, after they have known it, to turn from the holy commandment delivered unto them.[2]

It is the duty of every member of the Church, male and female alike, to search and obtain knowledge of the revealed truth. This will come through obedience to the commandments the Lord has given us. One of those commandments is that we should inform our minds and in the spirit of humility, obedience and faith, seek to know the will of the Lord, and to walk in spiritual light by obedience to every divine commandment.

Let us remember human nature has not changed since the day that men were first born into this mortal world. There have been down the corridor of time a few who were willing to keep the commandments of the Lord and who sought for light and truth. The great majority, however, followed the inclinations of the flesh as did the sons of Adam and Eve in the beginning. The enticements of a fallen world and the yielding to the weakness of the flesh have been powerful forces to lead mankind away from the divinely revealed truth. How true are the words recorded in the Book of Moses:

> And Adam and Eve blessed the name of God, and they made all things known unto their sons and their daughters.
>
> And Satan came among them, saying: I am also a son of God; and he commanded them, saying: Believe it not, and they believed it not, and they loved Satan more than God. And men began from that time forth to be carnal, sensual, and devilish.[3]

How greatly blessed the Latter-day Saints really are! We are living in the greatest dispensation of all time because it is the last for mortal souls. This dispensation is rapidly drawing to its close. Without ques-

---

[2]II Peter 2:20-21.
[3]Moses 5:12-13.

tion we are living as Elder Orson F. Whitney has written, in the Saturday evening of time.

This is a momentous period in this world's history because we are rapidly approaching the close of the Saturday night. Therefore it behooves members of the Church to watch and pray and through obedience prepare themselves for the glorious day which is soon to come when the cry will go forth: "Go Ye Out To Meet Him."

—JOSEPH FIELDING SMITH

1

This Life Is the Time for Men to Prepare to Meet God

Question: *"In Alma 34:31-34, we find the following: 'Yea, I would that ye would come forth and harden not your hearts any longer; for behold, now is the time and the day of your salvation; and therefore, if ye will repent and harden not your hearts, immediately shall the great plan of redemption be brought about unto you.*

" 'For behold, this life is the time for men to prepare to meet God; yea, behold the day of this life is the day for men to perform their labors.

" 'And now, as I said unto you before, as ye have had so many witnesses, therefore, I beseech of you that ye do not procrastinate the day of your repentance until the end; for after this day of life, which is given us to prepare for eternity, behold, if we do not improve our time while in this life, then cometh the night of darkness wherein there can be no labor performed.

" 'Ye cannot say, when ye are brought to that awful crisis, that I will repent, that I will return to my God. Nay, ye cannot say this; for that same spirit which doth possess your bodies at the time that ye go out of this life, that same spirit will have power to possess your body in that eternal world.'

"We have been discussing this statement, and we

wonder how it can be reconciled with the doctrine of salvation for the dead? It appears that those who have failed in this life are thus barred from any hope of salvation in the life to come. Why then, do we do temple work for the dead?"

Answer: This question presents a good illustration of the frequent difficulty into which so many fall when they have not carefully considered all the factors belonging to a subject. In the first place these people in the land of Antionum, known as Zoramites, had formerly been members of the Church and were dissenters from the Nephites. Amulek's remarks were intended as a plea for them to return to the Church and observe its covenants. He called their attention to the "many witnesses" that they had received and to forsake their evil ways before it was too late. They had departed from the commandments of the Lord and had violated his statutes, which they formerly believed, for a false system which denied the atonement of Jesus Christ. Therefore, the words of Amulek were timely. There was still hope for them if they would repent and turn back to the true faith and follow our Redeemer.

Worthy Entitled to Receive the Blessings

A word here in relation to those who are worthy to receive the blessings of the gospel but who died without the privilege, is necessary. Through the mercies of our Eternal Father and his Son Jesus Christ, it is decreed that every soul may have the privilege of hearing and embracing the truth. This is one of the glorious principles of the gospel, and one which the religious world has ignored. In giving his preface to the Doctrine and Covenants, the Lord said:

> For verily the voice of the Lord is unto all men, and there is none to escape; and there is no eye that shall not see, neither ear that shall not hear, neither heart that shall not be penetrated.
>
> And the rebellious shall be pierced with much sorrow; for their iniquities shall be spoken upon the housetops, and their secret acts shall be revealed.[1]

Therefore the promise is unto all who repent whether living or dead, that they shall not be deprived of the opportunity of hearing and accepting the truth. Therefore there must be a time for teaching the dead who died without the privilege of hearing and receiving the gospel when they were on the earth. This wonderful doctrine was revealed to the Prophet Joseph Smith, and he was given the divine authority to have the ordinances performed for the dead in the temples built for that purpose. This is a just principle filled with the spirit of mercy, love, and justice.

Every Soul Shall Have His Chance

That every soul shall have his chance is one of the greatest principles of the gospel. It is merciful and it is just, but these Zoramites could not see it because they had rebelled against the truth and had turned to the worship of false gods and thus had placed themselves on the border where there would be no hope if they continued in their evil course. So we see that there is no conflict between Amulek's teachings and the doctrine of the loss of salvation for the dead who turn away in this life and place themselves beyond hope of their

---

[1]D. & C. 1:2-3.

redemption. This condition which the Zoramites were in is in conformity to the condition of the apostates which Peter and Paul mention in their epistles as follows:

For it had been better for them not to have known the way of righteousness, than, after they have known it, to turn from the holy commandments delivered unto them.[2]

For it is impossible for those who were once enlightened, and have tasted of the heavenly gift, and were made partakers of the Holy Ghost,

And have tasted the good word of God, and the powers of the world to come,

If they shall fall away, to renew them again unto repentance; seeing they crucify to themselves the Son of God afresh, and put him to open shame.[3]

Status of Many Who Reject the Gospel

The Lord has not consigned all those who have rejected or may yet reject the gospel to the torments of the damned. He has decreed that every soul may have the opportunity of salvation in his kingdom if they will repent and keep his commandments. This applies as herein stated to all who died without any opportunity to repent and accept the gospel. According to that which is written, many of the honorable men who, when living, rejected the message of salvation who later in the world of spirits repented, will receive some degree of salvation. Of these the Lord has said:

And also they who are the spirits of men kept in prison, whom the Son visited, and preached the gospel unto them, that they might be judged according to men in the flesh;

---

[2]II Peter 2:21.
[3]Hebrews 6:4-6.

Who received not the testimony of Jesus in the flesh, but afterwards received it.

These are they who are honorable men of the earth, who were blinded by the craftiness of men.

These are they who receive of his glory, but not of his fulness.

These are they who receive of the presence of the Son, but not of the fulness of the Father.

Wherefore, they are bodies terrestrial, and not bodies celestial, and differ in glory as the moon differs from the sun.[4]

---

[4]D. & C. 76:73-78.

2

Prophets — Keys — Priesthood

Question: *"We have been discussing the coming of the Prophet Elijah, and a book we have states that he came because he holds the keys of the authority to administer in all the ordinances of the priesthood; and without that authority given, the ordinances could not be administered in righteousness.*

"One of the members referred to the Doctrine and Covenants and 'The Way To Perfection,' page 75, where it states that Moses and the Melchizedek Priesthood were taken from Israel, and yet we know that Samuel, Isaiah, Jeremiah, and Elijah, all held the Melchizedek Priesthood.

"How do we reconcile these two statements, and where do we get the scripture to prove that Elijah held all the keys of this authority to administer in all of the ordinances? If he held the keys of all the ordinances, then what about the ordinances of baptism and confirmation before he came? We understand that Christ instructed John to ordain Joseph Smith and Oliver Cowdery, and by that authority they baptized, but how does this conform to the statement made by the Prophet?"

Answer: The authority given to Elijah was that authority which pertains to the sealing ordinances of the gospel, such as we obtain in the temples of the Lord. Baptism was an ordinance introduced to Adam after he was driven out of the Garden of Eden and which could be performed by the authority of the Aaronic Priesthood, down through the ages. This authority was never taken away only through apostasy. Ordinances such as the Prophet mentioned were such as were received in sacred places which pertain to the Higher or Melchizedek Priesthood. The baptism by John was accepted by the Jews because they were familiar with this ordinance, notwithstanding the Bible, as it has come down to us, is so vague in relation to baptism for the remission of sin. The keys of the Melchizedek Priesthood were held by ancient prophets and by Israel's prophets until the time of Moses. When the Lord took these keys away from Israel and left them the Aaronic Priesthood, there was still the necessity for the Lord to maintain prophets who held the Melchizedek Priesthood, but they were especially called and ordained in each instance by the direct edict from the Lord.

All Priesthood Is Melchizedek

The Prophet Joseph Smith wrote:

> All Priesthood is Melchizedek, but there are different portions or degrees of it. That portion which brought Moses to speak with God face to face was taken away; but that which brought the ministry of angels remained. All the prophets had the Melchizedek Priesthood and were ordained by God himself.[1]

We discover that all the ordinances which could be performed by the Aaronic Priesthood remained with Israel in the dark days of her disobedience. It was necessary, under these conditions, that there be someone

---

[1] *Teachings of the Prophet Joseph Smith*, pp. 180-181.

with authority to perform ordinances, such as confirmation, for we know that the prophets of old had the gift of the Holy Ghost.[2]

We read in II Kings, Chapter 17, that power had been given to Elijah to close the heavens that there would be no rain except by his word. He had power given him to bless the widow's oil and meal and to bring down fire from heaven to consume his offering and destroy the false doctrines of the priests of Baal. The fact that Elijah had this great power and authority did not prevent other prophets from also holding some divine authority in the Melchizedek Priesthood which was essential to the faithful in the House of Israel. We should also remember the fact that in the days of the Savior's ministry this authority held by Elijah was bestowed by Elijah, and the authority held by Moses was restored by Moses to Peter, James, and John. In reference to this we have again the word of the Prophet Joseph Smith as follows:

The Priesthood Is Everlasting

The Priesthood is everlasting. The Savior, Moses and Elias, gave the keys to Peter, James, and John, on the mount, when they were transfigured before him. The Priesthood is everlasting —without beginning of days or end of years; without father, mother, etc. If there is no change of ordinances, there is no change of priesthood. Wherever the ordinances of the Gospel are administered, there is the Priesthood.[3]

Therefore, we discover that in the days of the Savior, he honored the prophets who held the keys of the priesthood in ancient times and called upon them

---

[2] II Peter 1:21.
[3] *Teachings of the Prophet Joseph Smith,* p. 158.

to come and bestow upon Peter, James, and John their keys, notwithstanding the fact that he held all the authority whence came the authority given to Moses and Elijah. It was also Moses and Elias (who lived in the days of Abraham) and Elijah who came to the Prophet Joseph Smith and Oliver Cowdery in the Kirtland Temple and again revealed their keys to be exercised in the Dispensation of the Fulness of Times.

It was Moses who held the keys of the gathering of Israel, and Elijah who held the keys of the turning of the hearts of the fathers to their children and the hearts of the children to their fathers, lest the Lord come and find the way unprepared.

Not only did these prophets come with their keys, but all of the prophets who held keys from Adam to Peter, James, and John, and John the Baptist also came with their keys and restored them that the Dispensation of the Fulness of Times might be complete preparatory to the coming of the Son of God as King of kings and Lord of lords, to take his place to rule and reign upon the earth according to the promise.[4]

---

[4]See D. & C. 128:18-21.

3

Salvation of Those Who Died without Law

Question: *"In the Doctrine and Covenants, Section 76, verse 72 there is a statement that those who die without law receive their place in the terrestrial kingdom. If this is true, how can there be hope in doing ordinance work for those who died without ever hearing about Christianity? If this applies only to the heathen nations, as some conclude, how can the Hawaiians, Japanese, Chinese, and others who never had a semblance of Christianity have work done for them?*

"Alma said: 'Yea, and I know that good and evil have come before all men; he that knoweth not good from evil is blameless; but he that knoweth good and evil, to him it is given according to his desires, whether he desireth good or evil, life or death, joy or remorse of conscience.' (Alma 29:5.)

"If the word of the Lord is law, then who are those who are spoken of in the Doctrine and Covenants?"

Answer: We may be sure that the Lord will deal righteously with all of his children, and that every soul will receive a just reward. The great object of this mortal life is that the spirits of men may obtain tabernacles of flesh and bones, for without these tabernacles the spirits of men could not rise to exaltation, neither could they be perfect without the union of flesh and bones with the eternal spirit. It was for this purpose that Adam and Eve were placed upon this earth and given the commandment to multiply.

After Adam was driven out of the Garden of Eden he was commanded to teach his children the full plan of salvation. In course of time they rebelled against God and were destroyed in the flood. Then the Lord commenced again with Noah and his family, and the same commandments were renewed. Like the antediluvians the descendants of Noah also rebelled, and idolatry came into existence, and the worship of many imaginary gods prevailed.

Loss of Divine Commandments Brought Wickedness

Eventually mankind was scattered over all the earth, and without divine commandments the knowledge of the gospel was lost, and depravity and wickedness prevailed. Some of these peoples sank into a condition not much better than the beast. As one generation followed another they became more depraved, and many lost all semblance of right and wrong, truth and righteousness.

We read in the Book of Abraham that the Lord revealed that in the world of spirits some of the intelligences were greater than others, and these he made his rulers. Contrariwise there were those who were less intelligent and evidently less fit for the exaltation offered to the faithful, yet these also were entitled to salvation from death and the torment of the damned. The Lord therefore had a place for these, thus showing his great mercy for all.

We learn from the word of the Lord to Moses that the Lord selected a place for the children of Israel, even before they were born, thus he indicated the number of spirits who were assigned to become the descendants of Jacob.[1] We may well believe that the Lord also parceled out the surface of the earth for all other peoples. Some of these places were evidently designed for inhabitants who had lost interest in or touch with the plan of salvation. We may well believe that the Lord did not permit the more progressive and more worthy spirits to come to the families of the ungodly and the less progressive peoples of the earth.

Mortality a Blessing and a Privilege

It was the privilege of this less progressive class, however, to come to the earth, and it was essential for them to receive the blessings of mortality. On this topic, however, there is very little revealed, but we may feel certain that it was essential that the more progressive and intelligent spirits were not sent to the tribes among the degraded heathen. These people naturally sank under such circumstances into a condition of ignorance and spiritual darkness. Children born under such circumstances could not be exalted, yet the Lord in his mercy had decreed to them to do the very best that could be done. Not having knowledge of the things of God, they were to be judged without law and assigned to a place after the resurrection that would be suited to them without the fulness promised to the faithful.

Revelation through Brigham Young

President Brigham Young, by revelation, received a clear view of this truth and has spoken of those who

[1] Deuteronomy 32:8-9.

are without law and understanding in the following words:

When God revealed to Joseph Smith and Sidney Rigdon that there was a place prepared for all, according to the light they had received and their rejection of evil and practice of good it was a great trial to many, and some apostatized because God was not going to send to everlasting punishment heathens and infants, but had a place of salvation in due time for all, and would bless the honest and virtuous and truthful, whether they belonged to any church or not. It was a new doctrine to this generation, and many stumbled at it.[2]

Again he said:

These words set forth the fact to which Jesus referred when he said, "In my Father's house are many mansions." How many I am not prepared to say; but there are three distinctly spoken of: the celestial, the highest; the terrestrial, the next below it; and the telestial, the third. If we were to take the pains to read what the Lord has said to his people in the latter days we should find that he has made provisions for all the inhabitants of the earth: every creature who desires, and who strives in the least, to overcome evil and subdue iniquity within himself or herself, and to live worthy of a glory, will possess one. We who have received the fulness of the gospel of the Son of God, or the kingdom of heaven, that has come to earth, are in possession of those laws, ordinances, commandments, and revelations, that will prepare us, by strict obedience, to inherit the celestial kingdom, to go into the presence of the Father and the Son.[3]

There are millions and millions of kingdoms that the people have no conception of. The Christians of this day have no knowledge of God, or godliness, or eternity, of the worlds that are, and that have been, and that are coming forth. There are myriads of people pertaining to this earth who will come up and receive a glory according to their capacity.[4]

---

[2] *Journal of Discourses* 16:42.
[3] *Ibid.*, 14:148.
[4] *Ibid.*, 6:347.

Some are not capable of the same exaltation as are others, arising from the difference of the conduct and capacities of people. There is also a difference in the spirit world. It is the design, the wish, the will, and mind of the Lord that the inhabitants of the earth should be exalted to thrones, kingdoms, principalities, and powers, according to their capacities. In their exaltation, one may be capable of presiding over more than five, another over only two, and another over but one. They must all first be subject to sin and to the calamities of mortal flesh, in order to prove themselves worthy; then the Gospel is ready to take hold of them and bring them up, enlighten their understandings, and make them one in the Lord Jesus, their faith, prayers, hopes, affections, and all their desires may ever be concentrated in one.[5]

Inspiration from President John Taylor

President John Taylor has added this enlightening thought:

There are heathen nations enveloped in idolatry; and if millions of people come into the world in these places surrounded with idolatry and superstition, it would be unjust for them to be punished for what they did not know, hence, if they have no law, they will be judged without law; and God in his own wisdom will regulate their affairs, for it is their misfortune, not their individual offense, that has placed them in their present position. If, however, we could trace their history, we should find, as with the Israelites, so with them. Their present darkness and misery originated in a departure from God; and as their fathers did not desire to retain God in their knowledge, he gave them up to the present darkness, confusion, and wretchedness. See Paul's remark on this subject in Romans 1:21-28. For naturally the conduct of fathers has a great influence over children, as well as in a family capacity. Hence the Jews will be blessed as a nation, in consequence of the promises made to Abraham, for as I have said before, these are eternal principles; man is an eternal being, and all his actions have relevancy to eternity. The

[5]*Ibid.*, 6:97.

actions of the fathers have a bearing and influence on their children both as families and nations, in time and in eternity.[6]

The Work of the Lord Is to Save

The great work of the Lord is to *save*, not *destroy*: therefore it is only the wilfully rebellious who have forsaken the truth who will eventually be cast out with the devil and his angels.[7]

All those who have lived upon the earth who have been subject to law and order and have had knowledge of good and evil and some understanding of the divine truth, although they have been steeped in the traditions of men, will be judged by the knowledge which they have. Among these there are many who were and are not Christians, but they were subject to law and order and had some divine understanding of justice and equity. These are worthy, on repentance, of salvation in the kingdom of God. It is for these that we do work in the temples that they may learn to live according to the laws of God and receive the blessings of his kingdom.

---

[6]*Government of God*, p. 52.
[7]D. & C. 76:31-38.

4

The Wearing of the Cross

Question: *"Having been reared in a Latter-day Saint community, I have never had occasion to give serious thought to this question of the wearing of the cross until I moved to the mission field.*

"Many who join the Church who come from a Catholic or Protestant background while trying their utmost to live the gospel, and rid themselves of past habits, unconsciously bring some of the customs of their former environment with them. One of these is the wearing of the crucifix on a necklace, bracelet, or in some other form.

"The teachings of The Church of Jesus Christ of Latter-day Saints seem to indicate that this is improper because we do not hold any special reverence for the cross as such, nor do we have crosses in our chapels or homes or wear a crucifix as jewelry. How may we uphold this belief, if my assumption is correct, through the study of the scriptures? Is there some statement that might be given from the General Authorities of the Church which would give me a clear understanding of this question?"

Answer: While we have never questioned the sincerity of Catholics and Protestants for wearing the cross, or felt that they were doing something which was wrong, it is a custom that has never appealed to members of the Church. The motive for such a custom by those who are of other churches, we must conclude, is a most sincere and sacred gesture. To them the cross does not represent an emblem of torture but evidently carried the impression of sacrifice and suffering endured by the Son of God. However, to bow down before a cross or to look upon it as an emblem to be revered because of the fact that our Savior died upon a cross is repugnant to members of The Church of Jesus Christ of Latter-day Saints.

The Cross Was an Egyptian Symbol

The use of the cross dates back to a very early time. Its early meaning is somewhat obscure. We are informed that the Egyptians used it as a symbol representing life and fertility of crops. However the general use throughout the Christian world comes from the crucifixion of our Redeemer. This custom of adoring the cross seems to have grown out of the purported vision given to Constantine when it is stated that he saw a cross in the heavens and was told that by it he was to conquer. From that time the use of the cross as an object of reverence grew, and when the rebellion against the Catholic Church commenced, the adoration of the cross continued more or less among the Protestant churches.

To many, like the writer, such a custom is repugnant and contrary to the true worship of our Redeemer. Why should we bow down before a cross or use it as a symbol? Because our Savior died on the cross, the wearing of crosses is to most Latter-day Saints in very poor taste and inconsistent to our worship. Of all the ways ever invented for taking life and the execution of individuals, among the most cruel is likely the cross. This was a favorite method among the Romans who excelled in torture. We may be definitely sure that if our Lord had been killed with a dagger or with a sword, it would have been very strange indeed if religious people of this day would have graced such a weapon by wearing it and adoring it because it was by such a means that our Lord was put to death.

A humble, contrite spirit and sincere prayer of gratitude is a far better means of worship and acknowledgment of our love for the great blessings we receive through our Savior's voluntary sacrifice than to adore the cross. It is through the shedding of his blood that we gain the resurrection; and by our faithfulness, exaltation in the kingdom of God.

5

Where Is the Garden of Eden?

Question: *"I am a stake missionary, and recently an investigator asked me the following question: 'I have found a contradictory statement in your teachings. The Bible says the Garden of Eden was in the Eastern Hemisphere, and the teachings of the Latter-day Saints say it was in the Western Hemisphere, in Missouri. How do you explain this?' I told her I would do some more checking and get an answer. You are no doubt familiar with the Bible quotation in Genesis 2:10-14, and I have checked the best I can but have not come up with anything definite enough to satisfy this investigator. Is there any geographical point that I could get that will bear this, our doctrine, out?"*

Answer: It is an error to say that the Bible states that the Garden of Eden was on the Eastern Hemisphere. The fact is that there is no place that can be definitely pointed out where the Garden of Eden was. There have been great changes on the face of the earth since the days of Adam. The Latter-day Saints would not know if the Lord had not revealed it to them. Such knowledge is beyond the skill of mortal man to discover without the revelation from the Lord.

Strange as it may seem, there is a popular view that the Garden of Eden was in the Mesopotamian Valley, not many miles from Mt. Ararat where the ark landed.

This view is inconsistent and contrary to the known facts as well as with the Bible. Some of these inconsistencies may be pointed out. The reason for the flood, as stated in the Bible, was to cleanse the earth of its iniquity which had become so great that the entire human family, excepting those who were saved in the ark, were destroyed. Another reason for the flood, as taught by revelation to the Church, is that the earth, like mankind, had to be baptized and purified by water. The scriptures state that the Lord opened the "fountains of the great deep" and "the windows of heaven," and caused it to rain incessantly until the entire earth was covered. The Latter-day Saints believe that this was the baptism of the earth.

The Cleansing of the Earth by Water

One or two quotations are given covering this point:

> The first ordinance instituted for the cleansing of the earth, was that of immersion in water; it was buried in the liquid element, and all things sinful upon the face of the earth were washed away. As it came forth from the ocean floor, like the new-born child, it was innocent; it rose to newness of life. It was its second birth from the womb of mighty waters—a new world issuing from the ruins of the old, clothed with all the innocence of this first creation.[1]

> The earth, in its present condition and situation, is not a fit habitation for the sanctified; but it abides the law of its creation, has been baptized with water, will be baptized by fire and the Holy Ghost, and by-and-by will be prepared for the faithful to dwell upon.[2]

---

[1]Orson Pratt, *Journal of Discourses*, Vol. I, p. 333.
[2]President Brigham Young, *ibid.*, 8:83.

Just where Noah built his ark is not known, but we are informed that it floated on the flood until the mountains were covered. It must have traveled a great distance from where it was built, for it would not remain still, and it was one hundred and fifty days at least floating before it settled at Mt. Ararat, in the upper country of Armenia. Now the ark no doubt was driven by the fierce winds which accompanied the flood. Out of the country where it rested, there flowed a river; it has been given the name Euphrates, but this river does not in the least correspond to the river by that name in the Garden of Eden. It was the most natural thing for Noah or some other ancient person, to name the river after the one which they had known, but this river flows in the wrong direction.

We call the river which flows from Utah Lake into the Great Salt Lake, the "Jordan," but that does not make it the river in Palestine, and what would be more natural than that the pioneers would call this stream, "Jordan?"

The Earth Has Undergone Many Changes

It should also be remembered that this good earth has passed through a great many changes since the days of Eden. The Bible teaches us that in the beginning all the water was in one place. Therefore all the land must have been in one place. (Genesis 1:9.) There *were not* an Eastern and a Western Hemisphere at the time of Adam. It is very strange, but nevertheless true, that some of the greatest events that have occurred on the face of the earth have been passed over in the Bible with the slightest mention; for example, in Genesis 10:25, we read:

"And unto Eber were born two sons: the name of one was Peleg; for in his day was the earth divided." This is a very brief statement of one of the greatest events that ever occurred on the face of this terrestrial globe, yet there is scientific evidence that this very thing happened. In the beginning the land surface was one vast continent; there came a time when it was divided, and other continents were formed and the Western Hemisphere came into existence, but this was long after the time of Adam.

Speaking of this great event Dr. Immanuel Velikovisky, in his book, *Earth in Upheaval,* makes the following comment:

> The theory of drifting continents, debated since the 1920's has its starting point in the similarity of the shape of the coastlines of Brazil and Africa. This similarity (or better, complementation) plus some early fauna and floral affinities suggested to Professor Alfred Wegner of Cruz in the Tyrol that in the early geological age these two continents, South America and Africa, were one land mass. But since animal and vegetable affinities, could also be found in other parts of the world, Wegner conjectured that all continents and islands were once a single land mass that in various epochs divided and drifted apart. Those who do not subscribe to the theory of continental drift continue to explain the affinity of plants and animals by "land bridges" or former land connections between continents and also between continents and islands.[3]

This, of course, has little to do with the Garden of Eden, but it does show that there have been great changes on the earth's surface since the days of Adam.

Other Scientists Testify to Earth's Change

Another scientific writer, Reginald Aldworth Daily,

[3]*Earth in Upheaval,* p. 118.

has written a large volume with the title *Our Mobile Earth* in which he argues that there have been great movements in the earth, and opposite page 260, he gives a diagram—three pictures—showing how at one time the land surface of the earth was in one place and how the scattered continents and islands could be brought back to one body of land, and how the continents "migrated" and separated from each other.

If one should take a map showing the Western and the Eastern hemispheres, and study them, one would see clearly how today they might be fitted together. Well, that day will come, for, as the earth was divided, so shall it in the restoration be brought back to its original form again, with all the land surface in one place. There are many prophecies in the Bible bearing on this union of continents and islands again. Here are a few of them:

> For this is as the waters of Noah unto me: for as I have sworn that the waters of Noah should no more go over the earth; so have I sworn that I would not be wroth with thee nor rebuke thee.
>
> For the mountains shall depart, and the hills be removed; but my kindness shall not depart from thee, neither shall the covenant of my peacc be removed, saith the Lord that hath mercy on thee.[4]
>
> For in my jealousy and in the fire of my wrath have I spoken, Surely in that day there shall be a great shaking in the land of Israel;
>
> So that the fishes of the sea, and the fowls of the heaven, and the beasts of the field, and all creeping things that creep upon the earth, and all the men that are upon the face of the earth, shall shake at my presence, and the mountains shall be

[4]Isaiah 54:9-10.

thrown down, and the steep places shall fall, and every wall shall fall to the ground.[5]

And every island fled away, and the mountains were not found.[6]

Then also the Lord revealed to the Prophet Joseph Smith the following in full accord with what is written in the Bible:

And he shall utter his voice out of Zion, and he shall speak from Jerusalem, and his voice shall be heard among all people;

And it shall be a voice as the voice of many waters, and as the voice of a great thunder, which shall break down the mountains, and the valleys shall not be found.

He shall command the great deep, and it shall be driven back into the north countries, and the islands shall become one land;

And the land of Jerusalem and the land of Zion shall be turned back into their own place, and the earth shall be like as it was in the days before it was divided.[7]

Our Knowledge Received through Revelation

We should be grateful to the Prophet Joseph Smith because of the revelation which the Lord gave to him pointing out the place of the Garden of Eden, and to give us the information that when the earth is restored, as it surely will be, the great city New Jerusalem will be in the place where Eden was.

---

[5]Ezekiel 38:19-20.
[6]Revelation 16:20.
[7]D. & C. 133:21-24.

6

When Did Jesus Appear to the Nephites?

Question: *"Several years ago I was asked to make a talk on the events which took place on the American continent at the first Easter. In studying for the talk I discovered that it was almost a year from the time that Christ was crucified until he showed himself to the Nephite multitude at the temple in the land Bountiful. 'And it came to pass in the thirty and fourth year, in the first month, there arose a great storm,' (III Nephi 8:5.) 'And it came to pass in the ending of the thirty and fourth year, behold, I will show unto you that the people of Nephi who were spared. . . .' (Ibid., 10:18.)*

"There is still a misconception of the event—or these events—in the minds of many of our members. Perhaps it doesn't really matter. Will you please discuss it?"

Answer: It is true that there has been a misconception in the minds of many members of the Church, but a careful reading of the account will clear up these misconceptions. It is true that a hasty examination will leave the impression that there was a delay of about a year after the resurrection of the Lord before he visited the Nephites and Lamanites who were spared; but more attention to what is written shows that it was but a very short time after his resurrection that the Lord appeared to the people who were assembled near the temple in Bountiful. This false conclusion that practically a year had passed from the time of the resurrection until the Lord appeared on this hemisphere has been published and circulated throughout the Church. Therefore we are justified in asking our brethren and sisters, and all who read the Book of Mormon, to pay close attention to the details of the story.

Destruction at the Time of the Crucifixion

In III Nephi 8:5, we discovered that in the "thirty and fourth year, in the first month, on the fourth day of the month, there arose a great storm, such an one as never had been known in all the land." The succeeding verses give much of the detail of the destruction which followed. This, evidently was at the time when Jesus was on the cross. Chapter 9 continues this story of destruction, and during this storm the voice of Jesus was heard in which he gave reasons for the great destruction, and he said:

> O all ye that are spared because ye were more righteous than they, will ye not now return unto me, and repent of your sins, and be converted, that I may heal you? . . .
>
> Behold, I am Jesus Christ the Son of God. I created the heavens and the earth, and all things that in them are. I was with the Father from the beginning, I am in the Father, and the Father in me; and in me hath the Father glorified his name.[1]

All of this was while the great darkness covered the earth, and Mormon then through the ninth and tenth chapters commented upon the terrible destructions which

---

[1]III Nephi 9:13, 15.

had taken place. He closes the tenth chapter in these words:

> And it came to pass that in the ending of the thirty and fourth year, behold, I will show unto you that the people of Nephi who were spared, and also those who had been called Lamanites, who had been spared, did have great favors shown unto them, and great blessings poured out upon their heads, insomuch that *soon after the ascension of Christ into heaven* he did truly manifest himself unto them—
>
> Showing his body unto them, and ministering unto them; and an account of his ministry shall be given hereafter. Therefore for this time I make an end of my sayings.[2]

Christ Appeared to Nephites Soon after Ascension

Here he declares that it was soon after the Savior's ascension into heaven that he appeared to the Nephites and Lamanites on this continent. And his ascension was the day of his resurrection after his appearance to Mary at the tomb, and before his appearance to the disciples that same day.

The reason why Mormon discontinued his account at this point is not stated. Evidently he was writing during the days of the great struggle with the Lamanites for the Nephite existence, and it is very possible that some sudden emergency had arisen so that he had temporarily to close his record. However, he continued his story where he broke off and states that there was a great multitude gathered together round about the temple in Bountiful. It seems perfectly clear that this great gathering was immediately after the close of the dreadful period of darkness. We read that the people were "marveling and wondering one with another," and

[2] *Ibid.*, 10:18-19; italics added.

"were showing one to another the great and marvelous change which had taken place."[3] While they were marveling and pointing out to each other these changes, and conversing, they heard a voice.

. . . it was not a harsh voice, neither was it a loud voice; nevertheless, and notwithstanding it being a small voice it did pierce them that did hear to the center, insomuch that there was no part of their frame that it did not cause to quake; yea, it did pierce them to the very soul, and did cause their hearts to burn.[4]

And it came to pass, as they understood they cast their eyes up again towards heaven; and behold, they saw a Man descending out of heaven; and he was clothed in a white robe; and he came down and stood in the midst of them; and the eyes of the whole multitude were turned upon him, and they durst not open their mouths, even one to another, for they thought it was an angel that had appeared unto them.[5]

Evidences for Appearances Following Resurrection

The fact that the multitude had gathered at the temple and were pointing out to each other the great changes that had occurred is evidence that this was an event immediately following the resurrection of our Lord. If this event had occurred one year later, the multitude would have been perfectly familiar with these great changes, and they would not have been so awed by them. It was in great astonishment and wonder that they had gathered and were pointing out to each other what had occurred.

Moreover it is contrary to reason that Jesus would make the Nephites and Lamanites, who had been faithful, wait for one whole year before he would make his

---

[3]*Ibid.*, 11:1.
[4]*Ibid.*, 11:3.
[5]*Ibid.*, 11:8.

appearance and give them instruction in relation to the closing of the period in which the law of Moses was in force, and the period when the fulness of the gospel was ushered in.

7

Is the Use of Ouija or Planchet Boards an Evil?

Question: *"It has come to our attention that some young people are amusing themselves with ouija and planchet boards. Our question is, Is the practice approved by the Authorities of the Church? It has always been our opinion that this was something of an evil nature in which the Spirit of the Lord had no part."*

Answer: The dictionary describes these boards as being for the purpose of "receiving answers to mediumistic communications or questions." This being the case, the answer is clear to your question. There can be no good or wholesome purpose accomplished in this kind of entertainment, therefore it should not be indulged in by members of the Church. The Lord has pointed out very clearly the course that we should take in obtaining inspiration for our guidance. When a person is baptized and receives the laying on of hands for the gift of the Holy Ghost, he is promised that he will receive the necessary guidance for his spiritual and temporal good, provided he is true to his covenants. The Lord will not dwell in unclean tabernacles. Therefore in order that we may keep ourselves in harmony with the Spirit of the Lord, we must be mentally, spiritually, and bodily clean from every contaminating influence.

In a revelation given to the Church in October 1830, the Lord said:

The Gift of the Holy Ghost Promised

Behold, verily, verily, I say unto you, this is my gospel; and remember that they shall have faith in me or they can in nowise be saved;

And upon this rock I will build my church; yea, upon this rock ye are built, and if ye continue, the gates of hell shall not prevail against you.

And ye shall remember the church articles and covenants to keep them.

And whoso having faith you shall confirm in my church, by the laying on of the hands, and I will bestow the gift of the Holy Ghost upon them.[1]

Shortly before Jesus departed from his apostles he gave them these instructions:

And I will pray the Father, and he shall give you another Comforter, that he may abide with you for ever;

Even the Spirit of truth; whom the world cannot receive, because it seeth him not, neither knoweth him: but ye know him; for he dwelleth with you, and shall be in you.[2]

Gift Promised to Each Church Member

This great gift is promised to each member of the Church who will be faithful and true, so there is no need for any member seeking inspiration or knowledge through any unsavory or evil source which is coming from Satan or one of his emissaries. Those who have

---

[1]D. & C. 33:12-15.
[2]John 14:16-17.

the light of the Spirit, or Holy Ghost, will avoid any contacts from any evil source. No doubt it is true that the use of these instruments is in the spirit of fun and for amusement. Let it be remembered that the Spirit of the Lord does not and will not dwell in unclean or disobedient tabernacles. When a person is enlightened by the teachings of the Spirit of the Lord, his whole soul is filled with peace, and an unmistakable joy beyond the power of description by mortal man. Moreover this great gift is offered to all members of the Church who consistently place their lives in harmony with the Holy Spirit.

There are some members of the Church who unfortunately refuse to comply with the commandments of the Lord, and this attitude deprives them of the guidance coming from the Holy Ghost. Therefore they are deprived of the great joy and peace of mind which a faithful life will bring. These souls are liable to deception. They fail to have the true discernment and are thereby deceived when some cunning person or spirit filled with the influence of the adversary of righteousness beguiles them into a false security. They become confused and many fall away from the Church into the depths of spiritual darkness. The disobedient and wayward become the prey of deception; and as darkness enters their souls, the true light is driven out.

Our Father Demands Obedience

Our Father in heaven has from the beginning demanded of his children that they love and obey him. They are to worship him, and unto him they are to pray and give their devotion. "He that seeketh me early shall find me, and shall not be forsaken," said the Lord.[3] To seek for information through ouija boards or any way contrary to the instruction the Lord has given is a sin. The Lord gave positive instruction to Israel when they were in the land of their inheritance that they were to go to him for revelation and to avoid the devices prevalent among the heathen nations who occupied their lands. The law of the Lord to Israel is drastic because the Lord considered it vital to their salvation. In the Book of Exodus, this is written:

> Thou shalt not suffer a witch to live.[4]
>
> And when they shall say unto you, Seek unto them that have familiar spirits, and unto wizards that peep, and that mutter: should not a people seek unto their God? for the living to the dead?[5]
>
> There shall not be found among you any one that maketh his son or his daughter to pass through the fire, or that useth divination, or an observer of times, or an enchanter, or a witch.
>
> Or a charmer, or a consulter with familiar spirits, or a wizard, or a necromancer.[6]

All through the Bible, the New Testament as well as the Old, the Lord and his prophets have expressed their displeasure when the people turned from the Lord to "familiar spirits." Even in our own day we have been given definite counsel in the following words:

> But ye are commanded in all things to ask of God, who giveth liberally; and that which the Spirit testifies unto you even so I would that you should do in all holiness of heart, walking uprightly before me, considering the end of your sal-

---

[3]D. & C. 88:83.
[4]Exodus 22:18.
[5]Isaiah 8:19.
[6]Deuteronomy 18:10-11.

vation, doing all things with prayer and thanksgiving, that ye may not be seduced by evil spirits, or doctrine of devils, or the commandments of men: for some are of men, and others of devils.

Wherefore, beware lest ye are deceived: and that ye may not be deceived seek ye earnestly the best gifts, always remembering for what they are given;

For verily I say unto you, they are given for the benefit of those who love me and keep my commandments, and him that seeketh so to do; that all may be benefited that seek or that ask of me, that ask and not for a sign that they may consume it upon their lusts.[7]

Counsel from President Joseph F. Smith

At the April conference, 1901, President Joseph F. Smith gave the following counsel to the members of the Church:

Men and women may be deceived by the craftiness of the adversary and by the spirit of darkness that is in the world; they may be deceived . . . with hypnotism, with animal magnetism, with mesmerism, with spiritualism and with all the other man-made and demon-stimulated isms which exist in the world; but the elect of God shall see and know the truth. They will not be blind, because they will see; they will not be deaf, because they will hear; and they will walk in the light, as God is in the light, that they may have fellowship with Jesus Christ, and that his blood may cleanse them from all their sins. May God help us to do this. May he deliver us from secret combinations, and from the snares that are set to entrap our feet and to win our affections from the kingdom of God. I repeat what I have said scores of times, the kingdom of God is good enough for me. This organization of The Church of Jesus Christ of Latter-day Saints meets all my wants, and I have no need to fly to organizations that are gotten up by men for the purpose of making money. I pray God that his kingdom may be sufficient

[7]D. & C. 46:7-9.

for you, that you may abide in the truth, and not be led away by these deceptive spirits that have gone forth in the world to lead men astray. Spiritualism started in the United States about the time that Joseph Smith received his visions from the heavens. What is more natural than that Lucifer should begin revealing himself to men in his cunning way, in order to deceive them and to distract their minds from the truth that God was revealing? and he has kept up pretty well ever since. May God bless Israel, and preserve us in the truth. . . ."

8

How Extensive Was the Scattering of Israel?

Question: *"My companion and I were discussing the lineage of the Israelites. I am a full blood Chinese, and have thought much of my lineage as mentioned in my patriarchal blessing. When I told my companion that my blessing said 'You are of the lineage of Abraham, Isaac, Jacob, and Ephraim,' he commented that I must not be pure Chinese. Since he has made such a statement, I have thought much about what is mentioned in the blessing. I will be grateful if you will inform me as to the relationship between races: Chinese, French, German, and others. I am particularly interested in this because I interpret the lineage literally and not as an adoption."*

Answer: Evidently the patriarch had the right interpretation. The great mission that was given to Abraham was that he would be a blessing to the generations coming after him, and through him all nations would be blessed. In Genesis we find the following:

> And I will make of thee a great nation, and I will bless thee, and make thy name great; and thou shalt be a blessing:
>
> And I will bless them that bless thee, and curse him that

curseth thee: and in thee shall all families of the earth be blessed.[1]

Again the Lord said:

> . . . Shall I hide from Abraham that thing which I do;
> Seeing that Abraham shall surely become a great and mighty nation, and all the nations of the earth shall be blessed in him?[2]

Great Blessings Promised Abraham's Seed

This wonderful promise is made in more detail in the writings of Abraham as we find them in the Pearl of Great Price:

> My name is Jehovah, and I know the end from the beginning; therefore my hand shall be over thee.
>
> And I will make of thee a great nation, and I will bless thee above measure, and make thy name great among all nations, and thou shalt be a blessing unto thy seed after thee, that in their hands they shall bear this ministry and Priesthood unto all nations;
>
> And I will bless them through thy name; for as many as receive this Gospel shall be called after thy name, and shall be accounted thy seed, and shall rise up and bless thee, as their father;
>
> And I will bless them that bless thee, and curse them that curse thee; and in thee (that is, in thy Priesthood) and in thy seed (that is, the Priesthood), for I give unto thee a promise that this right shall continue in thee, and in thy seed after thee (that is to say, the literal seed, or the seed of the body) shall all the families of the earth be blessed, even with the blessings of the Gospel, which are the blessings of salvation, even of life eternal.[3]

---

[1]Genesis 12:2-3.
[2]*Ibid.*, 18:17-18.
[3]Abraham 2:8-11.

When Israel entered the promised land, the Lord gave them strict commandment that they should serve him and keep his commandments. If they would obey, they were to be greatly blessed and prospered in the land the Lord had given to them. If they should reject his commandments and turn to evil, he would punish them and take them out of the land, and scatter them to all parts of the earth, where they would serve other gods, "which neither thou nor thy fathers have known, even wood and stone."[4]

All of this was to come on Israel as a punishment for their wickedness. However, the Lord never punishes his people without turning that punishment into some blessing in the end. The scattering of Israel became a blessing to the Gentile peoples among whom they were dispersed, for the Israelites mixed with the people thus bringing the Gentiles into the benefits of the blessings that had been promised to Abraham and his seed after him.

Most Latter-day Saints Are of Gentile Ancestry

Nearly all of the Latter-day Saints are of Gentile ancestry as well as being of the house of Israel. In the days of our Savior's ministry, he went only to the Israelites in Palestine, and when he sent his disciples out in the beginning, he commanded them not to go to the Gentiles but confine their labors to the Israelites in Palestine, and they obeyed this commandment.

We are all familiar with the difficulty Peter had accepting the pleadings of Cornelius to come into the Church, and in the first few years the preaching of the

[4]Deuteronomy 28:64.

gospel was confined to the Jews. It was only when the Jews rejected the message that Paul and his companions turned to the Gentiles.

A Significant Statement from the Book of Mormon

In this Dispensation of the Fulness of Times, the gospel came first to the Gentiles and then is to go to the Jews.[5] However, the Gentiles who receive the gospel are in the greater part, Gentiles who have the blood of Israel in their veins. There is a very significant statement in the words of Moroni as recorded on the title page of the Book of Mormon that it was: " . . . To come forth by the gift and power of God unto the interpretation thereof—Sealed by the hand of Moroni, and hid up unto the Lord, to come forth in due time by way of the Gentile —The interpretation thereof by the gift of God."

How did the Book of Mormon come forth? By the hand of Joseph Smith. Yet we read in the Book of Mormon[6] that Joseph Smith is the descendant of Joseph who was sold into Egypt by his brethren, nevertheless he came by "way of the Gentile," according to Moroni's prediction.

In the Book of Jacob, chapter five, in the Book of Mormon, we have one of the most remarkable parables ever written. It is the teaching of the Prophet Zenos and is related by Jacob. In this parable the house of Israel is represented as a tame olive tree which the Lord planted in his vineyard. The time came when the tree began to decay and the Lord pruned and nourished it, but the top began to perish. Then the Lord said,

---

[5]See D. & C. 19:27.

[6]See II Nephi 3:7-15.

It grieveth me that I should lose this tree; wherefore, go and pluck the branches from a wild olive-tree and bring them hither unto me; and we will pluck off those main branches which are beginning to wither away, and we will cast them into the fire that they may be burned.

And behold, saith the Lord of the vineyard, I take away many of these young and tender branches, and I will graft them whithersoever I will; and it mattereth not that if it so be that the root of this tree will perish, I may preserve the fruit thereof unto myself; wherefore, I will take these young and tender branches, and I will graft them whithersoever I will.

Take thou the branches of the wild olive-tree, and graft them in, in the stead thereof; and these which I have plucked off I will cast into the fire and burn them, that they may not cumber the ground of my vineyard. . . .

And it came to pass that the Lord of the vineyard went his way, and hid the natural branches of the tame olive-tree in the nethermost parts of the vineyard, some in one and some in another, according to his will and pleasure. . . .

And it came to pass that the Lord of the vineyard looked and beheld the tree in the which the wild olive branches had been grafted; and it had sprung forth and begun to bear fruit. And he beheld that it was good; and the fruit thereof was like unto the natural fruit.[7]

The Interpretation of the Parable

This is a very interesting parable, but what is here written will suffice. It reveals to us the fact that the Lord in scattering Israel to all parts of the world caused the branches of the tame olive tree and the wild olive tree, that had been grafted to bring forth fruit, while the main branches of the original olive tree had withered away.

The interpretation of this parable, and we have

[7]Jacob 5:7-9, 14, 17.

presented only a fragment of it, is a story of the scattering of Israel and the mixing of the blood of Israel with the wild olive trees, or Gentile peoples, in all parts of the world. Therefore we find in China, Japan, India, and in all other countries that are inhabited by the Gentiles that the blood of Israel was scattered, or "grafted," among them. Therefore in this day of gathering the Lord is fulfilling his purposes and is calling back into the fold of the True Shepherd, the children of Abraham. They are largely of the tribe of Ephraim, for Ephraim was given the blessing of standing at the head in the last days:

> And they, [that is, returning Israel,] shall bring forth their rich treasures unto the children of Ephraim, my servants.
>
> And the boundaries of the everlasting hills, shall tremble at their presence.
>
> And there shall they fall down and be crowned with glory, even in Zion, by the hands of the servants of the Lord, even the children of Ephraim.[8]

Therefore there is reason to believe the patriarch had the correct inspiration.

---

[8]D. & C. 133:31-33.

9

Is It a Sin to Kill Animals Wantonly?

Question: *"I am not writing this in criticism of the Church or even questioning whether the Church is right or wrong, but it is something I have wondered about for a long time. The scriptures seem clear to me that the Lord would rather not have man kill animals unless they are needed to sustain life; and in your 'Church History and Modern Revelation,' you present the same thought, even stating that killing for sport is a sin. I fully accept this as being true and have patterned my life accordingly. What I am wondering is why this is not generally taught here where so much hunting is done? I realize that many hunters eat what they kill; but to me this does not justify the killing just as a sport. I would appreciate it if you would express your thoughts on this subject."*

Answer: There is no statement in the scriptures indicating that the flesh of animals and birds and other living creatures was used as food before the days of Noah. It was after the landing of the ark that the Lord gave his commandment concerning the eating of flesh.

It reads in the King James version that this permission was given to Noah and those who came after as follows:

> And the fear of you and the dread of you shall be upon every beast of the earth, and upon every fowl of the air, upon all that moveth upon the earth, and upon all the fishes of the sea; into your hand are they delivered.
>
> Every moving thing that liveth shall be meat for you; even as the green herb have I given you all things.
>
> But flesh with the life thereof, which is the blood thereof, shall ye not eat.
>
> And surely your blood of your lives will I require; at the hand of every beast will I require it, and at the hand of man; at the hand of every man's brother will I require the life of man.[1]

The Lord revealed this in a different form to the Prophet Joseph Smith as follows:

INTERPRETATION FROM THE INSPIRED VERSION

> Every moving thing that liveth shall be meat for you; even as the green herb have I given you all things.
>
> But, the blood of all flesh which I have given you for meat, shall be shed upon the ground, which taketh life thereof, and the blood ye shall not eat.
>
> And surely, blood shall not be shed, only for meat, to save your lives; and the blood of every beast will I require at your hands.[2]

The inference in this interpretation is that the use of the flesh of living creatures should be indulged in sparingly although there was no sin in the shedding of their blood when required for food. There is no inference in the scriptures that it is the privilege of men to slay birds or beasts or to catch fish wantonly. The Lord gave

---

[1]Genesis 9:2-5.
[2]Holy Scriptures, Genesis 9:9-11. Inspired Version.

life to every creature, both the birds in the heavens, beasts on the earth, and the fishes in the streams or seas. They also were commanded to be fruitful and multiply and fill the earth. It was intended that all creatures should be happy in their several elements. Therefore to take the life of these creatures wantonly is a sin before the Lord.

It is easy to destroy life, but who can restore it when it is taken? Moreover, were not all creatures commanded to be happy in their spheres at least by implication if not by word? What a dreary world this would be should all life in the heavens above, on the earth, or in the sea be removed? What is more joyful to the ear than the voice of the robin on an early spring morning as he sings his song? The voice of the thrush, the meadow lark, even the bark of a friendly dog, each of them expressing their joy for their existence?

No! Man should be more the friend and never an enemy to any living creature. The Lord placed them here.

A Lesson as Taught by Joseph Smith

No doubt most of our readers have read the story of Zion's Camp on its fateful journey to the relief of their afflicted brethren. Even if you have, it is worth telling here. The Prophet Joseph Smith wrote:

> We crossed the Embarras river and encamped on a small branch of the same about one mile west. In pitching my tent we found three massasaguas, or prairie rattlesnakes, which the brethren were about to kill, but I said, "Let them alone—don't hurt them! How will the serpent ever lose his venom, while the servants of God possess the same disposition, and continue

to make war upon it? Men must become harmless, before the brute creation; and when men lose their vicious dispositions and cease to destroy the animal race, the lion and the lamb can dwell together, and the suckling child can play with the serpent in safety." The brethren took the serpents carefully on sticks and carried them across the creek. I exhorted the brethren not to kill a serpent, bird, or an animal of any kind during my journey unless it became necessary in order to preserve ourselves from hunger.

I had frequently spoken on this subject, when on a certain occasion I came up to the brethren who were watching a squirrel on a tree, and to prove them and to know if they would heed my counsel, I took one of their guns, shot the squirrel and passed on, leaving the squirrel on the ground. Brother Orson Hyde, who was just behind, picked up the squirrel, and said, "We will cook this that nothing may be lost." I perceived that the brethren understood what I did it for, and in their practice gave more heed to my precept than to my example which was right.[3]

Destruction of Animal Life Sometimes Necessary

We all realize that there are times when it is necessary to destroy animal life when it is the survival of the fittest, and they become a plague to mankind.

President Joseph F. Smith many years ago, gave to the youth of the Church this excellent counsel:

I have just a few words to say in addition to those that have already been said, in relation to shedding blood and to the destruction of life. I think that every soul should be impressed by the sentiments that have been spoken, and not less with reference to the killing of our innocent birds, natives of our country, who live upon the vermin that are indeed enemies of the farmer and to mankind. It is not only wicked to destroy them, it is abominable in my opinion. I think that this principle should extend, not only to the bird life, but to life of all animals. When I visited, a few years ago, the Yellowstone National Park,

[3]*DHC*, Vol. II, pp. 71-72.

and saw in the streams and the beautiful lakes, birds swimming quite fearless of man, allowing passers-by to approach them as closely almost as tame birds, and apprehending no fear of them, and when I saw droves of beautiful deer herding along the side of the road, as fearless of the presence of men as any domestic animal, it filled my heart with a degree of peace and joy that seemed to be almost a foretaste of that period hoped for when there shall be none to hunt and none to molest in all the land, especially among all the inhabitants of Zion. These same birds, if they were to visit other regions, inhabited by man, would, on account of their tameness, doubtless become more easily a prey to the gunner. The same may be said of those beautiful creatures—the deer and antelope. If they should wander out of the park, beyond the protection which is established there for these animals, they would become, of course, an easy prey to those who were seeking their lives. I never could see why a man should be imbued with a blood-thirsty desire to kill and destroy animal life. I have known men—and they still exist among us—who enjoy what is, to them, the "sport" of hunting birds and slaying them by the hundreds, and who will come in after a day's sport, boasting of how many harmless birds they have had the skill to slaughter, and day after day, during the season when it is lawful for men to hunt and kill (the birds having had a season of protection and not apprehending danger) go out by scores or hundreds, and you may hear their guns early in the morning on the day of the opening, as if great armies had met in battle; and the terrible work of slaughtering the innocent birds goes on.

I do not believe any man should kill animals or birds unless he needs them for food, and then he should not kill innocent little birds that are not intended for food for man. I think it is wicked for men to thirst in their souls to kill almost everything which possesses animal life. It is wrong. I have been surprised at prominent men whom I have seen whose very souls seemed to be athirst for the shedding of animal blood. They go off hunting deer, antelope, elk, anything they can find, and what for? "Just the fun of it!" Not that they are hungry and need the flesh of their prey, but just because they love to shoot and to destroy life. I am a firm believer, with reference to these things, in the simple words of one of the poets:

> "Take not way the life you cannot give,
> For all things have an equal right to live."[4]

And it shall come to pass, that before they call, I will answer; and while they are yet speaking, I will hear.

The wolf and the lamb shall feed together, and the lion shall eat straw like the bullock; and dust shall be the serpent's meat. They shall not hurt nor destroy in all my holy mountain, saith the Lord.[5]

Is it not an excellent time for man to set the example as the Prophet has said?

---

[4]*Gospel Doctrine,* "Man's Duty to Man."
[5]Isaiah 65:24-25.

10

What Was the Nature of Paul's Sin at the Stoning of Stephen?

Question: *"In our Sunday School the question of the nature and scope of Paul's sin at the martyrdom of Stephen was discussed. There was a wide divergence of opinion in the class. Some felt that he was justified by the teachings and policies of Jewish law. However some felt that it was in defiance of Roman law which was supreme at the time. Will you please help us to reach a proper conclusion?"*

Answer: Paul informs us that he was brought up in strict compliance with Israelitish law. He had been taught by the renowned Gamaliel who was known for his great wisdom and knowledge of Hebrew law. It is well for us to remember as far as we know that Paul took no part in making the decision that condemned Stephen and fortunately took no part in the stoning which cost Stephen his life. That he was in full sympathy with what was done we may well believe and therefore was willing to protect the clothes of those who engaged in the awful tragedy. It is likely true that he sanctioned the action. It is also true that in his misplaced zeal he was determined to bring all believers in Jesus to trial and have them punished perhaps to lose their lives by the violation of what he truly believed to be in full accord with the commandment of the Lord which had been given to Moses in relation to those who forsook the truth and turned to the worship of other gods.

Commandments Given to Ancient Israel Considered

In considering this let us refer to one or two passages in the commandments given to Israel when they entered the land of promise to inherit it.

> And the Lord spake to Moses, saying,
> Bring forth him that hath cursed without the camp; and let all that heard him lay their hands upon his head, and let all the congregation stone him. . . .
>
> And he that blasphemeth the name of the Lord, he shall surely be put to death, and all the congregation shall certainly stone him: as well the stranger, as he that is born in the land, when he blasphemeth the name of the Lord, shall be put to death.[1]
>
> If thy brother, the son of thy mother, or thy son, or thy daughter, or the wife of thy bosom, or thy friend, which is as thine own soul, entice thee secretly, saying, Let us go and serve other gods, which thou has not known, thou, nor thy fathers;
>
> Namely, of the gods of the people which are round about you, nigh unto thee, or far off from thee, from the one end of the earth even unto the other end of the earth;
>
> Thou shalt not consent unto him, nor hearken unto him; neither shall thine eye pity him, neither shalt thou spare, neither shalt thou conceal him:
>
> But thou shalt surely kill him; thine hands shall be first upon him to put him to death, and afterwards the hand of all the people.[2]

When we stop to consider that Paul was brought up in this atmosphere and that he was a very strict and

[1]Leviticus 24:13-14, 16.
[2]Deuteronomy 13:6-9.

devout Pharisee, we can understand how, in his ignorance, he was willing to take charge of the clothes of those who stoned Stephen. To him evidently it was a command from the Lord.

Hebrew Law Enforced against Stephen

While it is true that the Romans were in control and enforced their law, yet they did not always interfere with the Hebrew law and the carrying out of its provisions as understood by the Jews. In fact it is to be remembered that Pilate washed his hands and turned Jesus over to what he considered to be Hebrew law. Moreover let us not lose sight of the fact that Stephen was on trial before a council of the Jews.[3] The consigning him to death was not necessarily the work of a mob, but the action of the council, and Stephen, as was our Lord, supposedly, turned over to be dealt with according to Hebrew law.

At this condemnation of Stephen, as with Jesus, false witnesses were brought and were sworn who said that Stephen had, spoken " . . . blasphemous words against Moses, and against God,"[4] and when Stephen emphatically declared in their presence that he had seen the heavens opened and the Son of Man or Jesus standing on the right hand of God, it was more than these wicked judges could endure, and they pronounced sentence upon him, and the multitude cried out against him and cast him out of the city and stoned him.

Fortunately Paul took no part in this, only to take charge of the clothes of the guilty murderers. That he was sympathetic with them is true. Following this mur-

---

[3]Acts 6:12.
[4]*Ibid.*, 6:11.

derous assault he sought papers so that he could go forth arresting any who professed the name of Jesus and drag them to what he felt was justice. We must concede that in all that he did, Paul felt that he was doing what the Lord had commanded Moses in the law.

Paul Considered His Actions Were Justified

Under all the circumstances he was acting in righteous zeal, as he supposed, to bring to an end an uprising contrary to the commandment given by the Lord to Moses. In this mistaken zeal he went forth and " . . . made havock of the church, entering into every house, and haling men and women committed them to prison."[5]

To carry his labor to a complete conclusion, he sought papers so that he could go forth into other parts of the world, and on his way to Damascus received his great vision of the Son of God, which turned him from his bitterness and mistaken zeal to an equal zeal and determination henceforth to bring souls unto Christ.

Considering all the elements in connection with his life, we must say of Paul, what he did he did honestly in this work of destruction, feeling that he was doing the will of the Eternal Father. It was wrong, and it took a drastic measure to stop him in his mad course and turn him to the defense of the truth. Whatever evil was at his door, he fully paid the price through his greater zeal and perseverence to undo all that he had formerly done and bring souls unto Christ. Eventually it was required of him that he too lay down his life in martyrdom in defense of the Son of God whom previously he had persecuted.

---

[5]*Ibid.*, 8:3.

Surely Paul is worthy of our sympathy for the things he did which were wrong, and our love for his life of zeal which was intensified without question because of his evil labors ignorantly performed.

11

Our Responsibility to Warn the World

Question: *"A discussion came up in our seminary class yesterday. Just what is the responsibility of the Church in 'warning the world'?"*

Answer: Shortly before the betrayal of our Savior, he went out and sat on the Mount of Olives and his disciples came unto him privately and questioned him in regard to the destruction of the temple, the fate of the Jews, and his second coming and the end of the world, or the destruction of the wicked. Complying with their request the Lord revealed to them by prophecy all of these things. He told them they would go forth into the world and would be afflicted and hated by all nations for his name's sake. He told them how many who had professed his name would wax cold and would betray one another, but that he who remained steadfast and is not overcome, the same shall be saved.

In the course of his teaching he gave them some instruction concerning his second coming and said unto them:

> And again this gospel of the kingdom shall be preached in all the world, for a witness unto all nations, and then shall the end come, or the destruction of the wicked;
>
> And again shall the abomination of desolation, spoken of by Daniel the prophet, be fulfilled.

And immediately after the tribulation of those days, the sun shall be darkened, and the moon shall not give her light, and the stars shall fall from heaven, and the powers of heaven shall be shaken.

Verily, I say unto you, this generation, in which these things shall be shown forth, shall not pass away until all I have told you shall be fulfilled.

I have not taken this quotation from the Bible, but from the revelation given to the Prophet Joseph Smith as given in the Pearl of Great Price.[1] In the account given in Matthew and Luke the instruction reads as follows:

Verily I say unto you, This generation shall not pass, till all these things be fulfilled.[2]

Protestant Minister's Dilemma

This verse caused one minister in Chicago to write to other ministers in that great city, wherein he said he had no interpretation to give to this passage of scripture, for the generation in which our Lord lived passed away centuries ago, and yet this promise had not been fulfilled, and said he, "If we have no solution or sufficient answer to this statement, we might as well retire from the ministry for Christianity has failed."

One of these letters fell into my hands. What a wonderful difference a correct translation of the Savior's words can make, and how the members of the Church should rejoice and treasure the revelations coming through the Prophet Joseph Smith.

From the revelation given to the Prophet, Latter-

---

[1]Writings of Joseph Smith, 1:32-34.
[2]Matthew 24:34; Luke 21:32.

day Saints should be grateful, nevertheless we should take heed, for we are now living in the generation when these signs and warnings are made known. Therefore according to the words of the Savior's prophecy the time of his coming draws near. This truth all Latter-day Saints should realize, and we should be putting forth every effort to bring to pass the purposes of the Lord, one of the greatest being our responsibility to preach the gospel to the world.

In the discharge of this duty every member of the Church should be a missionary; not necessarily to go forth into the world, but to preach the gospel to our neighbors and friends who are not in the Church. Moreover, by our example and our faithfulness to every commandment the Lord has given us to show our friends and the strangers within our gates the way to eternal life through our actions as well as through our words, that is, to be humble missionaries and advocates of the truth in our daily acts and conversations.

Missionaries Are Fulfilling Commandment

Today the missionaries of the Church are fulfilling this commandment by going forth in all countries where the doors are open, preaching the gospel, and crying repentance to the people, and bearing testimony of the restoration of the gospel. In doing so there are certain commandments missionaries should remember. First, that they are sent not only to preach and bear testimony and bring people to repentance preparatory to the second coming of the Lord and the establishment of his kingdom to rule and reign in the earth, but to warn all men by virtue of that divine authority which is in them. Those who heed their teachings and repent will come into the

Church and be numbered among those who have received the covenants of the gospel. Those who refuse to hear are to be left without excuse, for the Lord has declared it in the following words:

> Behold, I sent you out to testify and warn the people, and it becometh every man who has been warned to warn his neighbor.
>
> Therefore, they are left without excuse, and their sins are upon their own heads.[3]
>
> *And again, by way of commandment to the church concerning the manner of baptism*—All those who humble themselves before God, and desire to be baptized, and come forth with broken hearts and contrite spirits, and witness before the church that they have truly repented of all their sins, and are willing to take upon them the name of Jesus Christ, having a determination to serve him to the end, and truly manifest by their works that they have received of the Spirit of Christ unto the remission of their sins, shall be received by baptism into his church.[4]

Missionaries should also remember that before a person is baptized he or she should subscribe to the covenant of baptism as the Lord has given it by revelation.

---

[3]D. & C. 88:81-82.
[4]*Ibid.*, 20:37.

12

The Debt We Owe

Question: *"There seems to be much misunderstanding in the world as to the nature of the atonement of Jesus Christ and our indebtedness to him for making possible the resurrection. Will you please clarify the Church's view on this subject?"*

Answer: One of the most enlightening discourses ever delivered in regard to the atonement is found in the ninth chapter of II Nephi in the Book of Mormon. It is the counsel given by Jacob, brother of Nephi. It should be carefully read by every person seeking salvation. We have been taught that the greatest gift of God is eternal life, and eternal life comes through obedience to all of the commandments and covenants given to man by our Heavenly Father.

There is an overwhelming lack of understanding in the world in relation to these principles of salvation and exaltation given to prepare mankind for a place in the kingdom of God, and this lack causes many to stumble. There is no excuse on the part of members of the Church, for they have received the necessary revelation directly from the heavens in this Dispensation of the Fulness of Times. The great mission of the Son of God has been revealed in the Book of Mormon and the Doctrine and Covenants more clearly than any other place. Many passages that have been misunderstood, and therefore mistranslated in the Bible, are clarified in these sacred volumes.

The Blessing of Immortality and Eternal Life

The greatest debt we owe is to our Redeemer, Jesus Christ, for the great blessings of immortality and eternal life. Immortality is the gift vouchsafed to every soul, for the edict has gone forth from the throne of God that the resurrection must be just as broad as the fall. Adam was the person who brought death into the world, and no member of his family is held accountable for death and therefore will receive the resurrection. It is through the love and mercy of the Son of God for humanity that this redemption comes. His extreme suffering and cruel death upon the cross brought to pass the atonement for Adam's transgression and redeems every creature who partook of the fall from the grave, including his bitter enemies who cried out against him—"Let him be crucified!" Yes, they also are beneficiaries of the atonement and shall receive the resurrection although they will likewise suffer for their dreadful sin.

Let us reflect on some of the great truths portrayed in Jacob's message which was written, not only for his own people but for the benefit of the entire world.

> For as death hath passed upon all men, to fulfil the merciful plan of the great Creator, there must needs be a power of resurrection, and the resurrection must needs come unto man by reason of the fall; and the fall came by reason of transgression; and because man became fallen they were cut off from the presence of the Lord.
>
> Wherefore, it must needs be an infinite atonement—save it should be an infinite atonement this corruption could not put on incorruption. Wherefore, the first judgment which came upon

man must needs have remained to an endless duration. And if so, this flesh must have lain down to rot and to crumble to its mother earth, to rise no more.[1]

Death Is a Merciful Plan

Before continuing with this discourse, let us pause and consider the expression that death comes to fulfil the "merciful plan of the great Creator."

Many mortals do not believe that death is a merciful plan. It is the prevalent belief that Adam committed a dreadful sin in partaking of the forbidden fruit. Commentators have written that this act was "man's shameful fall," as though through partaking of the fruit Adam and Eve brought into the world a condition of misery and death that could have been avoided; and Adam and his posterity could have lived in peace, love, and contentment, free from death had not they transgressed. Mother Eve had revealed to her the true purpose for the fall wherein she said:

> . . . Were it not for our transgression we never should have had seed, and never should have known good and evil, and the joy of our redemption, and the eternal life which God giveth unto all the obedient.[2]

The fall therefore was a necessary part of the plan of salvation, and Jacob speaks of it as a "merciful plan of the Creator." Surely no one wishes to remain in mortality when he becomes old and helpless. Death comes to all as a merciful, and not a fearful thing, especially to the person who dies with the assurance of a righteous resurrection.

---

[1]II Nephi 9:6-7.
[2]Moses 5:11.

Lehi, father of Jacob, informs us that "Adam fell that men might be; and men are, that they might have joy."[3]

Fall Brought Privilege of Mortal Existence

The fall of Adam and Eve gave the human race the privilege of mortal existence which otherwise they would not have received. Thus all the experiences gained in mortality would have been lost to us if this divine plan had not been adopted.

We must not think that the death of the body is the end of man and that when we die the body returns to the earth to rise no more. Jacob has pointed out clearly what the consequences would have been if the physical death were the end of the mortal body, and how the Father had prepared the way for man's redemption, through the atonement of Jesus Christ. This redemption was the plan adopted before the foundation of the earth.

> O the wisdom of God, his mercy and grace! For behold, if the flesh should rise no more our spirits must become subject to that angel who fell from before the presence of the Eternal God, and became the devil, to rise no more.
>
> And our spirits must have become like unto him, and we become devils, angels to a devil, to be shut out from the presence of our God, to remain with the father of lies, in misery, like unto himself; yea, to that being who beguiled our first parents, who transformeth himself nigh unto an angel of light, and stirreth up the children of men unto secret combinations of murder and all manner of secret works of darkness.
>
> O how great the goodness of our God, who prepareth a way for our escape from the grasp of this awful monster; yea,

---

[3]II Nephi 2:25.

that monster, death and hell, which I call the death of the body, and also the death of the spirit.

And because of the way of deliverance of our God, the Holy One of Israel, this death, of which I have spoken, which is the temporal, shall deliver up its dead; which death is the grave.

And this death of which I have spoken, which is the spiritual death, shall deliver up its dead; which spiritual death is hell; wherefore, death and hell must deliver up their dead, and hell must deliver up its captive spirits, and the grave must deliver up its captive bodies, and the bodies and the spirits of men will be restored one to the other; and it is by the power of the resurrection of the Holy One of Israel.[4]

Main Purpose for Mortal Existence Explained

What could be more dreadful than such a fate as that the body should be eternally destroyed, and the spirit be left as it was before the mortal life? What could have been gained? Yet there are many who have departed from the teachings of the Savior who deny the resurrection. The main purpose for our mortal existence is that we might obtain tabernacles of flesh and bones for our spirits that we might advance after the resurrection to the fulness of the blessings which the Lord has promised to those who are faithful. They have been promised that they shall become sons and daughters of God, joint heirs with Jesus Christ, and if they have been true to the commandments and covenants the Lord has given us, to be kings and priests and queens and priestesses, possessing the fulness of the blessings of the celestial kingdom.

This great promise was made to the spirits of men before the foundation of the earth was laid. The Lord

[4] *Ibid.*, 9:8-12.

has renewed this promise to us if we will patiently endure the ills of the flesh as well as receive the blessings and go through the trials and tribulations faithfully to the end.

Our Redeemer so loved the world that he volunteered to come and suffer by the shedding of his blood and thus pay the debt of the fall and make it possible for every soul to gain a place in his celestial kingdom. No one can fully realize the price that Jesus paid to make our salvation and exaltation possible. He has described it in the following words:

> For behold, I God, have suffered these things for all, that they might not suffer if they would repent;
>
> But if they would not repent they must suffer even as I;
>
> Which suffering caused myself, even God, the greatest of all, to tremble because of pain, and to bleed at every pore, and to suffer both body and spirit—and would that I might not drink the bitter cup, and shrink—
>
> Nevertheless, glory be to the Father, and I partook and finished my preparations unto the children of men.[5]

Christ Redeemed Every Soul

Is it possible to think of any fate that would be as terrible as to be denied the resurrection, our spirits becoming subject to Satan forever? How grateful to our Redeemer every soul should be to think that Jesus so loved the world that he was willing to suffer and redeem every soul from death and give us the resurrection of the dead. Surely every member of the Church of Jesus Christ should be willing to show gratitude by obedience to the Savior's commandments.

---

[5]D. & C. 19:16-19.

No mortal can fully realize the price that he paid. No mortal could have stood the anguish and suffering of such a sacrifice. It was a sacrifice that a God had to endure. It is an insignificant price we are asked to pay, and we should be willing to pay it in the spirit of thanksgiving, love, and obedience to every divine command. As he loves us, so we should love him, showing our deep gratitude in obedience and in humble prayer.

13

Differences in Bodies in the Resurrection

Question: *"The Lord has revealed through the Prophet Joseph Smith that there will be no marriage outside of the celestial kingdom, and even there, only among those who have been faithful to all covenants in mortal life and have been married according to divine law in the temple of the Lord. The question was raised in our class in regard to men and women who are assigned to other kingdoms, also those who are in the celestial kingdom and who are unmarried; what will prevent them from living together outside of the marriage covenant? We assume it to be a fact that females, as well as males, in great numbers will inherit places in these other kingdoms.*

"Will you kindly discuss this problem for us?"

Answer: We may well believe that our Eternal Father has fully considered this point and made ample provision to meet the situation. In the Doctrine and Covenants, Section 88, we are informed that there will be differences in the bodies of inhabitants of the several kingdoms to meet every need and restriction.

And they who are not sanctified through the law which I have given unto you, even the law of Christ, must inherit another kingdom, even that of a terrestrial kingdom, or that of a telestial kingdom.

For he who is not able to abide the law of a celestial kingdom cannot abide a celestial glory.

And he who cannot abide the law of a terrestrial kingdom cannot abide a terrestrial glory.

And he who cannot abide the law of a telestial kingdom cannot abide a telestial glory; therefore he is not meet for a kingdom of glory. Therefore he must abide a kingdom which is not a kingdom of glory.[1]

All Individuals to Receive Resurrection

We are informed in this revelation that those who cannot abide any of these kingdoms will also be quickened, that is they will receive the resurrection, but they shall go to their own place, " . . . to enjoy that which they are willing to receive, because they were not willing to enjoy that which they might have received."[2]

Since bodies will be raised in the resurrection to suit the condition of each individual, the Lord will assign each man and woman to the place which each has earned. We are fully justified in believing that provision has been made to cover every emergency and condition peculiar to each kingdom. Our own judgment should reveal to us that our Father in heaven would not overlook a matter as vital as this fact that men and women are to be assigned to the several kingdoms which their mortal lives entitle them to obtain. Divine justice will be meted out to each, whether male or female, according to their opportunities to hear and receive his gospel, and based on their free agency to act independently of the commandments and blessing of the Lord. As simple a matter as marriage for eternity and the union of the sexes

---

[1]D. & C. 88:21-24.
[2]*Ibid.,* 88:32.

in eternity has been determined according to the mercy and justice of our Eternal Father. We may conclude that the matter of the sexes was fully considered and the decree entered long before the Garden of Eden or the time when this earth was formed.

Orson Pratt's Explanation

Elder Orson Pratt in a wonderful discourse on the resurrection has given this key to the situation, which must be true, for it seems clear and logical:

> In all the works of God, we behold a resemblance among classes; but a variety among individuals belonging to each class. All the planets of our system resemble each other more or less in form; but in magnitude and many other respects, there is a great variety. In every species of animals and plants, there are many resemblances in the general outlines, and many specific differences characterizing the individuals of each species. So in the resurrection: there will be several classes of resurrected bodies; some celestial, some terrestrial, some telestial, and some sons of perdition. Each of these classes will differ from the others by prominent and marked distinctions; yet many resemblances as well as distinctions. There will be some physical peculiarity by which each individual in every class can be identified.[3]

Our own sober judgment teaches us that the Lord in his infinite wisdom and justice, would see to it that the privileges of increase or cohabitation between men and women in these kingdoms would be impossible because of peculiar conditions pertaining to these glories.

Is not the sectarian world justified in their doctrine generally proclaimed, that after the resurrection there will be neither male or female sex? It is a logical conclusion for them to reach and apparently is in full har-

---

[3]*The Seer*, p. 274.

mony with what the Lord has revealed regarding the kingdoms into which evidently the vast majority of mankind is likely to go. However, if members of the Church are faithful and true to the covenants and commandments of the gospel, there is no reason for them to worry about the condition which will prevail in these several kingdoms.

14

In Obeying God, Is Personal Liberty Curtailed?

Question: *"Our class recently discussed the subject of obedience in all things, and in the course of the discussion these words of Seneca were considered:*

" 'We are born subjects, and to obey God is perfect liberty. He that does this shall be free, safe, and happy.'

"We disagreed with the phrase, 'perfect liberty.' We seek your advice on this question. How could there be perfect liberty if we are compelled to accept the same view, and individuality and freedom of expression are denied? We ask you to answer in terms of Church philosophy. Is not this an interference with personal freedom and the right of a person to express his own thoughts on many subjects? Will you give us an answer based in terms of gospel philosophy?"

Answer: Seneca (Lucius Annaeus) was a Roman writer and philosopher who lived in the first century of the Christian era. It is unlikely that he ever saw the Lord, but there is a tradition that he had some acquaintance with Paul and from him may have absorbed some gospel truth. Whether this is true or not cannot be definitely stated. This expression which is here called in question by members of the class is one of considerable importance.

We have all been taught the doctrine of personal free agency and that no individual is ever compelled by force or other means to comply with divine edicts and philosophy. We have been informed that a long time ago in the pre-existence there was a rebellion in heaven, and because one notable character, who had been entrusted with great authority, rebelled and led many away with him, he had to be cast out of the kingdom. However we should remember that every principle and law existing in the celestial kingdom has been proved to be perfect through the eternities through which they have come. If any individual proves himself worthy for the exaltation in that kingdom, it will be by strict obedience to every principle and covenant here existing. Therefore we may be assured that every law and principle thereunto pertaining is perfect and cannot be amended or discarded because of its perfection. However there is no reason to believe that under such conditions there could arise differences of judgment or opinion in relation to any principle or commandment, for everything has reached the stage of perfection.

All Divine Laws Have Been Thoroughly Tested

We may well believe that since our Eternal Father has been building worlds, peopling them, and having them go on to perfection through countless ages, that every divine law and commandment has been so thoroughly tested that there could not come at any time a condition where an individual who reaches the exaltation could discover wherein any principle or commandment could be discarded or in any way amended to improve the conditions of that kingdom.

One of the most glorious principles or truths ever revealed to mortal man was given to the Prophet Joseph Smith in Kirtland, Ohio, in May 1831. This truth, for some reason which is difficult to explain, has been criticized by many who ought to know better, but it stamps Joseph Smith as a prophet and a revelator who has made known to the world perhaps one of the greatest truths that was ever revealed. Yet the world will not receive it! Unfortunately many who profess membership in the Church have questioned the validity of it. It is as follows:

> And that which doth not edify is not of God, and is darkness.
>
> That which is of God is light; and he that receiveth light *and continueth in God,* receiveth more light; and that light groweth brighter and brighter until the perfect day.[1] (Italics added.)

There is another revelation similar to this, which points to the time when all who find that divine light and truth will be exalted. It is as follows:

> The Spirit of truth is of God. I am the Spirit of truth, and John bore record of me, saying: He received a fulness of truth, yea, even of all truth.
>
> And no man receiveth a fulness unless he keepeth his commandments.
>
> He that keepeth his commandments receiveth truth and light, until he is glorified in truth and knoweth all things.[2]

---

[1]D. & C. 50:23-24.
[2]*Ibid.*, 93:26-28.

Worthy to Be Blessed in Knowledge and Wisdom

Here we are informed that those who are worthy of the exaltation will be blessed in knowledge, wisdom, truth, and light, so that they will, like our Lord, eventually know all things and be bathed in light and truth. When this time comes there could not arise any differences of opinion. There could be no ambitious souls who would be dissatisfied, or who would wish to introduce any individual notions or wish to change the laws by which all things in perfection are governed. Since the joy of all who dwell there is perfect there could arise no occasion for a difference of opinion or a conflict of ideas. The weakness and imperfections of mortality will all be brushed aside, and those who receive this exaltation will be bathed in wisdom, light, and truth in their perfection.

Should there arise a person or persons who wish to change the order, then the perfect order would cease to exist. Neither could any person or group discover any principle or commandment that would need to be modified, for the eternal state of perfection has been reached.

True freedom can only come through obedience to divine law. This is true in this mortal world; how much more so in the celestial kingdom. There is no compulsion there. Every soul who reaches this exaltation will realize that there could be no disharmony, and when the inhabitants of that kingdom see clearly, and not "through a glass darkly," there will arise no contention. Personal ambitions are due to mortal desires. In the kingdom of God those who enter will have learned the great lessons of humility, obedience, and divine love, for all the weaknesses and ambitions of the flesh will have perished with the grave.

It Is Possible to Attain Perfection

The Savior's words in the Sermon on the Mount, "Be ye therefore perfect, even as your Father which is in heaven is perfect,"[3] evidently have been by many misapplied or limited in their application. The Savior knew that mortal man could not reach the great goal of perfection like his Heavenly Father, but here in mortality is the place where that foundation should be laid. Then we should continue on from grace to grace, not only in this life but also in the eternities to come, and it is within the possibility of any faithful soul eventually to attain to that perfection.

Again:

> Then said Jesus to those Jews who believed on him, If ye continue in my word, then are ye my disciples indeed:
>
> And ye shall know the truth, and the truth shall make you free.[4]

True freedom can come only through obedience to divine law. There is no compulsion in the kingdom of God. Wisdom, love of truth, and obedience make us free. The moment a person turns from the path of truth and observance of divine law, he becomes subject to sin and a slave to sin. There is more truth in the words of James than many think:

> For whosoever shall keep the whole law, and yet offend in one point, he is guilty of all.[5]

---

[3]Matthew 5:48.
[4]John 8:31-32.
[5]James 2:10.

What is the true meaning of this remark? It is that only by obedience to the full law, can the promised blessings come.

The purpose of our mortal existence is that each individual may be tried and tested to see if, through the temptations, trials, and tribulations of mortality, he can maintain a faithful demeanor and prove himself worthy of the exaltation in the kingdom of God. This is the goal we are seeking or should seek, and it is this integrity and perseverence which brings the fulness of life which Lehi has defined as joy.

15

What of the Dead Who Died before Jesus Christ?

Question: *"In the fifteenth chapter of Mosiah we read that those who lived before the coming of our Savior, who never heard of him and never had salvation declared to them had part in the first resurrection at the time the Savior arose, and have eternal life. Will you please enlighten us in regard to this as we wonder how and why this could be, without their having heard the message of the gospel when living in this world?"*

Answer: This question is in reference to the teachings of Abinadi as follows:

And there cometh a resurrection, even a first resurrection; yea, even a resurrection of those that have been, and who are, and who shall be, even until the resurrection of Christ—for so shall he be called.

And now, the resurrection of all the prophets, and all those that have believed in their words, or all those that have kept the commandments of God, shall come forth in the first resurrection; therefore, they are the first resurrection.

They are raised to dwell with God who has redeemed them; thus they have eternal life through Christ, who has broken the bands of death.

And these are those who have part in the first resurrection;

and these are they that have died before Christ came, in their ignorance, not having salvation declared unto them. And thus the Lord bringeth about the restoration of these; and they have a part in the first resurrection, or have eternal life, being redeemed by the Lord.[1]

Children Are Not Answerable for Sins of Parents

The millions of souls who have lived on the earth at a time and place when the gospel was not here, due to the transgressions of their fathers, cannot be judged by the standards which the pure gospel proclaims. Many of the people living in the pagan world were intelligent, industrious, honest in their dealings with their fellows, but were unfortunate to be descendants of those who in earlier ages rejected the gospel which had been declared to them, and therefore their descendants were raised in idolatry. The Lord declared through his prophets that the children are not answerable for the sins of their parents.

> The fathers shall not be put to death for the children, neither shall the children be put to death for their fathers: every man shall be put to death for his own sin.[2]

After the scattering of the people to all parts of the earth, they fell away from the teachings of Noah. Generation after generation came and passed in idolatry. Yet many of these children were otherwise intelligent. They had accepted the worship of images and false gods because of the traditions of their fathers. Among these peoples were many of the Egyptians, the Greeks, the Romans, the Persians, and peoples who had spread out all over the face of the earth. These people were not

[1]Mosiah 15:21-24.
[2]Deuteronomy 24:16.

responsible for their condition. They had followed the teachings of their fathers and lived and died in their ignorance of divine truth taught to Adam, to Noah, and to Abraham.

Justice Will Be Meted Out to Every Soul

We are taught that we will be punished for our own sins, but what of these millions who sinned ignorantly, not having any knowledge of the mission of the Son of God? According to the divine plan the truth of the gospel must eventually be declared to them, for it is written that " . . . the voice of the Lord is unto all men, and there is none to escape; and there is no eye that shall not see, neither ear that shall not hear, neither heart that shall not be penetrated."[3]

So we discover that the Lord, in his great mercy, will remember the heathen as well as Israel, and that justice will be meted out to every soul. We have the assurance that every soul who was ignorant of the truth when living shall have the gospel taught to him, although it may be delayed to the days when he is in the spirit world.

We are taught that people cannot be punished for what they did not know. Therefore Abinadi said of those who died in their ignorance:

> And these are those who have part in the first resurrection; and these are they that have died before Christ came, in their ignorance, not having salvation declared unto them. And thus the Lord bringeth about the restoration of these; and they have a part in the first resurrection, or have eternal life, being redeemed by the Lord.[4]

---

[3]D. & C. 1:2.
[4]Mosiah 15:24.

To Be Judged By Intent of Heart

We are taught that mankind through the ages will be judged by the privileges and opportunities to know the truth. If a person never had the opportunity to know anything about the plan of salvation, then surely he should not be held accountable for his deeds in the flesh on an equality with the man who knew the truth and then refused to obey it. Thousands of these people who lived in this ignorance were devout and faithful to the doctrines which they had been taught. They cannot be held accountable for their actions which were done in faith and obedience to that which they devoutly believed and had been taught.

Fortunately the Lord will judge us all by the intent of the heart as well as by our understanding. Therefore it seems that it was only a matter of justice for the Lord to do what Abinadi said he would do and permit these who innocently died in "their ignorance, not having salvation declared unto them" to have part in this great resurrection. The question naturally arises: Little children who do not understand, should they die, are they redeemed through the blood of Christ? The scriptures inform us also that this is the privilege of all those who are without law:

> For behold that all little children are alive in Christ, and also all they that are without the law.[5]

A Glorious Principle of Truth and Justice

We may be sure that the Lord would do all things according to the law of eternal justice and that he would

[5]Moroni 8:22.

not punish people who in ignorance sinned and violated his commandments. It is one of the most glorious principles of truth and justice that was ever revealed that men are to be punished according to their disobedience to divine commandments, but not when they have acted innocently in ignorance of those divine edicts.

Think of the poor Lamanites converted by Ammon, Aaron, and their brethren. They had been guilty of many serious transgressions, murdering their "enemies" the Nephites, for no apparent cause, but, when the truth penetrated their souls, and they truly and humbly repented, they were forgiven, and the light of the gospel entered their souls.

One thing we should remember in reading what Abinadi said and that is this:

> But behold, and fear, and tremble before God, for ye ought to tremble; for the Lord redeemeth none such that rebel against him and die in their sins; yea, even all those that have perished in their sins ever since the world began, that have wilfully rebelled against God, that have known the commandments of God, and would not keep them; these are they that have no part in the first resurrection.[6]

---

[6]Mosiah 15:26.

16

Was the Fall of Adam Necessary?

Question: *"In our discussion of the fall of Adam the question arose: the first commandment given to Adam and Eve was to multiply and the second that they should not eat the fruit of the tree of the knowledge of good and evil or they would die. The discussion presented the fact that the two commandments were in conflict, and by breaking the commandment not to eat the fruit, Adam and Eve had to die. The thought was also expressed that we could all be in a state of innocence but for the fall. We would like to have a clear explanation of this. Surely the Lord would not permit his plan to be destroyed."*

Answer: It is evident that if we were dependent solely on the account of the fall as it is presented in the Book of Genesis, we would be led astray and reach a very erroneous conclusion. The Bible has come to us through many translations, and there is no original known to man. In the copying of the ancient records and the translations by uninspired men, many errors crept into the ancient writings. The Book of Mormon makes this clear. This has led Bible commentators to speak of Adam and Eve as having frustrated and defeated the original plan of the Father, and they have spoken of the partaking of the fruit as

"Man's Shameful Fall." Therefore there is a prevalent notion that if Adam and Eve had not partaken of this fruit, they and their posterity would have dwelt upon the earth in perfect peace and happiness without the trials and temptations that have become so prevalent through the generations of time, and there would have been no death.

The Fall Was Essential to the Divine Plan

The simple fact is, as explained in the Book of Mormon and the revelations given to the Prophet Joseph Smith, the fall was a very essential part of the divine plan. Adam and Eve therefore did the very thing that the Lord intended them to do. If we had the original record, we would see the purpose of the fall clearly stated and its necessity explained. We do have this knowledge in the Book of Moses as it was revealed to the Prophet Joseph Smith as follows:

> And I, the Lord God, commanded the man, saying: Of every tree of the garden thou mayest freely eat,
>
> But of the tree of the knowledge of good and evil, thou shalt not eat of it, nevertheless, thou mayest choose for thyself, for it is given unto thee; but, remember that I forbid it, for in the day thou eatest thereof thou shalt surely die.[1]

We learn from this that Adam had the privilege of making a choice, with the penalty of death awaiting him if he ate the fruit of the tree. We may assume that Adam would not have eaten if Eve had not partaken. When she did, Adam realized that he had to partake or he and Eve would have been separated forever.

[1]Moses 3:16-17.

Therefore there was nothing left for Adam to do but to follow Eve's example and partake.

We read also in the scriptures that Jesus was the "Lamb slain from the foundation of the world," meaning that our Savior was chosen before the foundations of the world to come and be the sacrifice for the redemption of man and all the creatures who partook of death through Adam's fall.

Original Account Found in Book of Moses

Just why the Lord would say to Adam that he forbade him to partake of the fruit of that tree is not made clear in the Bible account, but in the original as it comes to us in the Book of Moses it is made definitely clear. It is that the Lord said to Adam that if he wished to remain as he was in the garden, then he was not to eat the fruit, but if he desired to eat it and partake of death he was at liberty to do so. So really it was not in the true sense a transgression of a divine commandment. Adam made the wise decision, in fact the only decision that he could make.

It was the divine plan from the very beginning that man should be placed on the earth and be subject to mortal conditions and pass through a probationary state as explained in the Book of Mormon where he and his posterity would be subject to all mortal conditions. It was part of the divine plan that man should have this period of mortality where he would be shut out of the presence of God and be subject to all the vicissitudes of mortality, the temptations and trials of the flesh, thus gaining experience and being placed in a position of trial, temptation, and be purified by passing through the trials and tribulations of the flesh, or mortality, as Paul has described it. This life is a very brief part of our existence, but is the most critical, for it is in mortality where we are tried and figuratively placed in the fire and tested, proved to see what kind of material we are made of, whether we will be worthy of an exaltation in the kingdom of God or be assigned to some other kingdom.

Adam's Transgression Explained by Prophet Lehi

Lehi, in instructing his son Jacob, made this very clear wherein he said:

> And now, behold, if Adam had not transgressed he would not have fallen, but he would have remained in the garden of Eden. And all things which were created must have remained in the same state in which they were after they were created; and they must have remained forever, and had no end.
>
> And they would have had no children; wherefore they would have remained in a state of innocence, having no joy, for they knew no misery; doing no good, for they knew no sin.
>
> But behold, all things have been done in the wisdom of him who knoweth all things.
>
> Adam fell that man might be; and men are, that they might have joy.
>
> And the Messiah cometh in the fulness of time, that he may redeem the children of men from the fall. And because that they are redeemed from the fall they have become free forever, knowing good from evil; to act for themselves and not to be acted upon, save it be by the punishment of the law at the great and last day, according to the commandments which God hath given.[2]

---

[2]II Nephi 2:22-26.

Mother Eve has given us the clearest statement in relation to the fall in the following words:

> . . . Were it not for our transgression we never should have had seed, and never should have known good and evil, and the joy of our redemption, and the eternal life which God giveth unto all the obedient.[3]

---

[3]Moses 5:11.

17

What Is the Sin against the Holy Ghost?

Question: *"What I am asking may not be of any importance, but perhaps you can inform me as to where I may find information on the subject. I am puzzled in my mind about the word 'blasphemy' as stated in Matthew 12:31-33. It tells us that to blaspheme against the Son of Man can be forgiven, but to blaspheme against the Holy Ghost can never be forgiven. Through what kind of action or means would one go about to blaspheme against the Holy Ghost? Perhaps if I could read a good article on this subject I could form a conclusion."*

Answer: You have asked a very important question, which may be difficult to explain to a person who is not a member of The Church of Jesus Christ of Latter-day Saints or to one who has been inactive and indifferent to the teachings of the Church.

In order to have the question clearly before us it is well to quote the passage in question.

> Wherefore I say unto you, All manner of sin and blasphemy shall be forgiven unto men; but the blasphemy against the Holy Ghost shall not be forgiven unto men.
>
> And whosoever speaketh a word against the Son of man, it shall be forgiven him: but whosoever speaketh against the Holy Ghost, it shall not be forgiven him, neither in this world, neither in the world to come.

> Either make the tree good, and his fruit good; or else make the tree corrupt, and his fruit corrupt: for the tree is known by his fruit.[1]

THE GIFT OF THE HOLY GHOST

When John the Baptist was preaching in the wilderness he said to the people:

> I indeed baptize you with water unto repentance: but he that cometh after me is mightier than I, whose shoes I am not worthy to bear: he shall baptize you with the Holy Ghost, and with fire.[1]

On several occasions the Savior spoke to his disciples about the gift of the Holy Ghost. This gift is spoken of frequently in the Bible, particularly in the New Testament.

When Nicodemus came to the Savior seeking light, the Lord said to him:

> Verily, verily, I say unto thee, Except a man be born of water and of the Spirit, he cannot enter into the kingdom of God.[2]

This was a strange saying to Nicodemus, so he asked how could a man be born again, and the Lord answered:

> Verily, verily, I say unto thee, Except a man be born of water and of the Spirit, he cannot enter into the kingdom of God.
>
> That which is born of the flesh is flesh; and that which is born of the Spirit is spirit.
>
> Marvel not that I said unto thee, Ye must be born again.

---

[1]Matthew 12:31-33; 3:11.
[2]John 3:5.

The wind bloweth where it listeth, and thou hearest the sound thereof, but canst not tell whence it cometh, and whither it goeth: so is every one that is born of the Spirit.[3]

The Birth of Water Is Baptism by Immersion

The birth of water is of course baptism by immersion for the remission of sins. This is an essential ordinance for entrance into the kingdom of God.

The baptism of the Spirit is by the laying on of hands by one who holds the priesthood.

No man is authorized to perform these ordinances unless he holds the priesthood. An ordinance performed by one who has not received authority would be only a mockery in the sight of the Lord. Likewise the gift of the Holy Ghost is conferred by the laying on of hands by one who has been officially invested with divine authority. Joseph Smith and Oliver Cowdery received this authority from Peter, James, and John who were sent to confer upon them the Melchizedek Priesthood. The Lord said to Joseph Smith in a revelation given in October 1830:

Yea, repent and be baptized, every one of you, for a remission of your sins; yea, be baptized even by water, and then cometh the baptism of fire and of the Holy Ghost.

Behold, verily, verily, I say unto you, this is my gospel; and remember that they shall have faith in me or they can in nowise be saved;

And upon this rock I will build my church; yea, upon this rock ye are built, and if ye continue, the gates of hell shall not prevail against you.

---

[3]*Ibid.*, 3:5-7.

And ye shall remember the church articles and covenants to keep them.

And whoso having faith you shall confirm in my church, by the laying on of the hands, and I will bestow the gift of the Holy Ghost upon them.[4]

Paul Questions Validity of Ephesian Baptisms

Paul realized that something was wrong when certain converts at Ephesus claimed to have been baptized, and he asked them if they had received the Holy Ghost since being baptized. They replied, "We have not so much as heard whether there be any Holy Ghost."

From this answer Paul had grave doubts concerning the validity of their baptism, and he asked them, "Unto what then were ye baptized?" They answered, "Unto John's baptism." Then Paul said, "John verily baptized with the baptism of repentance, saying unto the people, that they should believe on him which should come after him, that is, on Christ Jesus." When they heard this, they were baptized in the proper manner, for Paul knew that their baptism had been without divine authority. Paul then laid his hands upon them and gave them the gift of the Holy Ghost, and the power thereof came upon them, "and they spake with tongues and prophesied."[5]

This gift was held by all the prophets of old as Peter informs us wherein he said:

Knowing this first, that no prophecy of the scripture is of any private interpretation.

---

[4]D. & C. 33:11-15.
[5]See Acts 19:1-6.

For the prophecy came not in old time by the will of man: but holy men of God spake as they were moved by the Holy Ghost.[6]

Members of The Church of Jesus Christ of Latter-day Saints, through their faithfulness and integrity, are entitled to the same guidance and divine knowledge which was given to the Saints in other dispensations from the days of Adam down. However, no person can have this gift and exercise faith, unless he or she is humbly keeping the commandments the Lord has given. The Holy Ghost will not dwell in unclean tabernacles nor strive with people unless they keep their minds as well as their bodies clean, and they are diligent before the Lord.

When the Savior met with his apostles in solemn assembly shortly before his betrayal he said to them:

If ye love me, keep my commandments.

And I will pray the Father, and he shall give you another Comforter, that he may abide with you for ever;

Even the Spirit of truth; whom the world cannot receive, because it seeth him not, neither knoweth him: but ye know him; for he dwelleth with you, and shall be in you.[7]

Nevertheless I tell you the truth; It is expedient for you that I go away: for if I go not away, the Comforter will not come unto you; but if I depart, I will send him unto you.

And when he is come, he will reprove the world of sin, and of righteousness, and of judgment:

Of sin, because they believe not on me;

Of righteousness, because I go to my Father, and ye see me no more;

Of judgment, because the prince of this world is judged.

---

[6]II Peter 1:20-21.
[7]John 14:15-17.

I have yet many things to say unto you, but ye cannot bear them now.

Howbeit when he, the Spirit of truth, is come, he will guide you into all truth: for he shall not speak of himself; but whatsoever he shall hear that shall he speak: and he will shew you things to come.

He shall glorify me: for he shall receive of mine, and shall shew it unto you.[8]

The World Is Bereft of the Holy Ghost

The world today does not have this great gift because men have forsaken the way of the Lord, have discarded his ordinances, and teach the philosophies of men.

The Lord will grant to any honest person who earnestly seeks to know the truth *one* manifestation by the Holy Ghost; but he is not entitled to repeated manifestations. After such a revelation is given, he is to act, for the Holy Ghost cannot be appealed to for continued manifestations until after baptism and the gift has been bestowed. Cornelius is a good example of this. Peter was holding strictly to the traditions of Israel that the fulness of the gospel was for Israel only and not for the Gentiles. The Lord gave him a strange vision before he was convinced that the gospel was for the Gentiles as well as for the Jews.

We learn from the inspired teachings of Moroni the following:

Behold, I would exhort you that when ye shall read these things, [i.e., the Book of Mormon] if it be wisdom in God that ye should read them, that ye would remember how merciful

[8]*Ibid.*, 16:7-14.

the Lord hath been unto the children of men, from the creation of Adam even down until the time that ye shall receive these things, and ponder it in your hearts.

And when ye shall receive these things, I would exhort you that ye would ask God, the Eternal Father, in the name of Christ, if these things are not true; and if ye shall ask with a sincere heart, with real intent, having faith in Christ, he will manifest the truth of it unto you, by the power of the Holy Ghost.

And by the power of the Holy Ghost ye may know the truth of all things.[9]

The Constant Companionship of the Holy Ghost

So important is the gift of the Holy Ghost that through righteous, humble obedience to the gospel a person will have the constant companionship of the Holy Ghost. The discernment of spirits and the power to understand and clearly comprehend the revelations of the Lord will be given him. What a glorious privilege this is to be guided constantly by the Holy Ghost and to have the mysteries of the kingdom of God made manifest.

How can one read the epistles of Paul or Peter or any of the prophets of old and not understand how these men were in possession of divine authority and that their minds were enlightened by the teachings and revelations of the Holy Ghost? It is because of this glorious contact that a person may receive and know with all his soul that Jesus is the Christ and that his prophets have spoken the truth; also by his inward testimony which the Spirit has given.

After this revelation is given should a man turn

[9]Moroni 10:3-5.

away and deny the truth? It would be with his eyes open and the knowledge that the Holy Ghost had given him of divine truth. Hence he would prove himself to be a liar and unworthy of a place of salvation in the kingdom of God. The testimony that comes of the truth is so great through the teachings of the Holy Ghost that the punishment for a rebellion or sin against the Holy Ghost merits a punishment where there is no forgiveness.

Paul, in writing to the Hebrews gave this warning:

For it is impossible for those who were once enlightened, and have tasted of the heavenly gift, and were made partakers of the Holy Ghost,

And have tasted the good word of God, and the powers of the world to come,

If they shall fall away, to renew them again unto repentance; seeing they crucify to themselves the Son of God afresh, and put him to an open shame.[10]

Peter Also Bears His Testimony

Peter also bears his testimony to the truth that there is no forgiveness for the man who sins against the Holy Ghost.

For if after they have escaped the pollutions of the world through the knowledge of the Lord and Saviour Jesus Christ, they are again entangled therein, and overcome, the latter end is worse with them than the beginning.

For it had been better for them not to have known the way of righteousness, than, after they have known it, to turn from the holy commandment delivered unto them.

But it is happened unto them according to the true proverb,

---

[10]Hebrews 6:4-6.

the dog is turned to his own vomit again; and the sow that was washed to her wallowing in the mire.[11]

The testimony of the Spirit is so great, and the impressions and revelations of divine truth so forcefully revealed that there comes to the recipient a conviction of the truth that he cannot forget. Therefore, when a person once enlightened by the Spirit so that he receives knowledge that Jesus Christ is the Only Begotten Son of God in the flesh, then turns away and fights the Lord and his work, he does so against the light and testimony he has received by the power of God. Therefore, he has resigned himself to evil knowingly. Therefore Jesus said there is no forgiveness for such a person.

The testimony of the Holy Ghost is the strongest testimony that a man can receive.

---

[11]II Peter 2:20-22.

18

Nephite Baptisms and the Gift of the Holy Ghost

Question: *"Jesus said to the Nephites that he would baptize with fire and the Holy Ghost, but the statement seems to indicate that such baptism was done without the laying on of hands. In the Book of Mormon it indicates that Jesus baptized the Lamanites in a similar way, and administered to them, but still the practice of laying on of hands for the bestowal of the Holy Ghost is not mentioned. We always lay on hands for the bestowal of the Holy Ghost, and in spite of the rule the Savior said to Nephi: 'I will baptize with fire and with the Holy Ghost.' Will you kindly give an explanation of this?"*

Answer: It is true that the Lord gave the commandment to Joseph Smith that those who are baptized for the remission of sins shall receive the gift of the Holy Ghost by the laying on of hands, and this is the practice in the Church. This does not prove, however, that the gift of the Holy Ghost may not be received without the laying on of the hands, although we assume that this was the general custom of the Church in ancient days.

When certain disciples were brought to Paul at Corinth who claimed that they had been baptized, he asked them the question: "Have ye received the Holy

Ghost since ye believed?" Their answer was: "We have not so much as heard whether there be any Holy Ghost." Paul then asked: "Unto what then were ye baptized?" They answered, "Unto John's baptism." Paul realized from this answer that there was something wrong, therefore he had them baptized again, after which he laid his hands upon them and conferred the Holy Ghost.[1] This, however, may not have been the universal custom through the ages.

When Jesus was with his disciples, he said to them, shortly before his crucifixion:

> If ye love me, keep my commandments.
>
> And I will pray the Father, and he shall give you another Comforter, that he may abide with you forever;
>
> Even the Spirit of truth; whom the world cannot receive, because it seeth him not, neither knoweth him: but ye know him; for he dwelleth with you, and shall be in you.[2]
>
> Howbeit when he, the Spirit of truth, is come, he will guide you into all truth: for he shall not speak of himself; but whatsoever he shall hear, that shall he speak: and he will shew you things to come.[3]

THE LORD'S PROMISE TO HIS DISCIPLES

In these words the Savior promised his disciples that they would be blessed with the gift of the Holy Ghost when he departed from them and before he took his departure the record states that he " . . . breathed on them, and saith unto them, Receive ye the Holy Ghost."[4]

---

[1]See Acts 19:2-6.
[2]John 14:15-17.
[3]*Ibid.*, 16:13.
[4]*Ibid.*, 20:22.

Evidently this was just as efficient as if he had laid his hands upon them.

We discover in the reading of the scriptures that the Lord conferred authority on some of his chosen servants and gave them exceptional powers without the laying on of hands, but merely by his spoken edict. In this manner Elijah obtained the keys of power in the priesthood to raise the dead, heal the sick, close the heavens that it did not rain only by his word, and for more than three years there was no rain, and moreover he had the power to call down fire from heaven to destroy the enemies of the Church.

Speaking of this, James has said:

> Elias was a man subject to like passions as we are, and he prayed earnestly that it might not rain: and it rained not on the earth by the space of three years and six months.[5]

The Lord May Bestow Gift by Other Means

The Lord gave similar authority to Nephi, son of Helaman, who likewise had authority to close the heavens and perform other mighty works, simply by his faith and the commandment from the Lord.[6] This wonderful power has been bestowed on but a few of the servants of the Lord.

We may correctly believe that the Lord may bestow the gift of the Holy Ghost by other means than by the laying on of hands if occasion requires it. While it is the practice to lay on hands, there are many incidents recorded in the scriptures where divine authority has been bestowed by the divine edict to the prophets. In

---

[5] James 5:17.
[6] Helaman 10:7.

the case of the assembled multitude near the temple at the time of the appearing of the Lord, we also read that angels descended and encircled the little ones and ministered to them.

Now a careful reading of the first chapters in III Nephi reveal to us that Nephi, grandson of Helaman, with other faithful brethren, labored diligently among the people before the crucifixion of the Lord. They baptized all who humbled themselves and repented of their sins. They had power to confirm, to heal, and even to raise the dead, but after the crucifixion of the Savior there came a new order of things. The law of Moses came to an end, and with it, sacrifice of animals ceased, and the fulness of the gospel was ushered in. Therefore in this new order it became necessary for all those who had been previously baptized to be baptized again.

Nephites Had Authority to Officiate

Nephi and his fellow servants had been, no doubt, baptized and confirmed, otherwise they could not have given service in the authority of the priesthood, and they could not have performed the miracles that had been accomplished. The condition among the Nephites and Lamanites was exactly the same as that which existed just before the organization of the Church in April, 1830. Quite a number of brethren and sisters had been baptized, including of course Joseph Smith and Oliver Cowdery, who were baptized at the direction and commandment of John the Baptist before there was a Church. Baptism is also then entrance into the Church as well as for the remission of sins. Therefore in the new order, Jesus commanded Nephi to be baptized and also the other brethren of the twelve. Following this all of the people were baptized. The conferring of the gift of the Holy Ghost would naturally follow, except in the case of those who had been previously baptized and confirmed.

We may be sure that Jesus did not overlook any ordinance that was necessary when he visited the children of Lehi after his resurrection. His visitation to these people was a glorious occasion, and we learn from what is written that these people of that generation remained faithful and true all the days of their lives, walking in the spirit of faith and humility and guided by the blessings coming through the gift of the Holy Ghost.

19

Why Was Not Paul Ordained by Peter to the Apostleship?

Question: *"Why was not Paul ordained to the apostleship by Peter, James, and John, who were apostles? In reading the first chapter of Paul's epistle to the Galatians, we find this: 'Paul, an apostle, not of man, neither by man, but by Jesus Christ, and God the Father, who raised him from the dead.'*

"In verses 15 and 16, Paul points out that when God called him he did not confer with flesh and blood, neither did he go up to Jerusalem to them that were apostles before him, but he went into Arabia. It was three years before he went to Jerusalem, and then the only apostles he saw were Peter and James, the Lord's brother. Leaving Jerusalem he went to Syria and Cilicia, and the Churches of Judea not having seen him by face, only heard that he now preached the faith which once he destroyed.

"Fourteen years later Paul and Barnabas (who was an apostle) and Titus went to Jerusalem, and Paul communicated with them in a conference. But when they saw that the gospel of the circumcision was committed to Peter, then James, Cephas, and John gave Paul and Barnabas the right hand of fellowship and agreed that Paul and Barnabas would go to the heathen. Now we are wondering if a new dispensation of the gospel was

committed to Paul. There are scriptures that seem to support this thought."

Answer: Unfortunately the records that have come down to us are extremely fragmentary. We have no continuous story. Paul became an eye-witness to the mission of the Lord when he received the great vision which turned him from his mistaken course. This, however, did not constitute the qualification for the apostleship. There were a number of things that had to be done. First, he had to be baptized for the remission of his sins and confirmed; then he went into retirement in Arabia, no doubt for a period of study and preparation and prayer. He then returned to enter the ministry with humility and zeal, surpassing the efforts of many of the brethren. There is no doubt that he spent some time with the brethren in which he convinced them of his integrity and his complete conversion to the mission of the Son of God.

Historical Details only Fragmentary

We are extremely lacking in information in relation to many important details that failed to seep through the ages to our day, and we are left in darkness to know when and where Paul was ordained. But this is not strange when we think of the fragmentary information that has been received.

There is no written record as to when Barnabas became an apostle, or James, the brother of the Lord.

If it had not been for the faithful recording by Luke, the chances are that we would have as little about the activities of Paul as we have about Peter and John and the other original members of the council of apostles. The fact may be correctly surmised that Paul did find time to mingle with his brethren and that through the divine inspiration the apostleship was conferred on him by their action. It is evidently true also that Barnabas likewise was by them ordained; also James, the Lord's brother, and others if we had the record. We have no reason to believe that Paul received his ordination independent of the action of the other apostles.

Nothing Strange in Paul's Statement

There is nothing strange in his statement in the introduction in his epistle to the Galatians, or to the Corinthians, Ephesians, Colossians, and Timothy, that his call was *not* of man, but of God. Just when and how he was ordained is not revealed, but this is true of Barnabas. What does matter is the fact that Paul, like Peter, James, and John, and the other apostles, received authority by a divine call. Not one of them obtained the authority by the will of man! We all could wish that more had been revealed, but the Lord has sanctioned their ministry, and we know it is true.

James, the brother of John, we know was cut down in martyrdom after a very brief ministry. Our knowledge of the activities of others of the original twelve is clouded in mystery; that they were faithful is true, and indications point to the fact that all of the original twelve and also Paul, laid down their lives in martyrdom, except John the Revelator, and he was spared to continue his ministry until the second coming of our Lord, according to the revelation given to Nephi six hundred years before John's birth.

It Is Easy for One to Be Misled

It is very easy for one to be misled and reach a false conclusion in relation to these apostles and their ministry because of the lack of authentic information. We learn more of the journeying and ministry of Paul because he had an excellent scribe with him in his missionary labors. It is evident that the original twelve had but few occasions, during their ministry, to meet in council. Conditions were vastly different in that day from the conditions which prevail today. When Paul and Barnabas, or Silas and other brethren, went forth among the nations they had to go on foot, occasionally by donkey and when crossing the Mediterranean, by ship, but whatever means, it was a laborious and tedious journey. They had no means of communication except by letter, usually carried by a friend. Paul on several occasions writes of sending in the care of friends information and greetings to others. Peter refers to Paul's ministry in the following words:

> Wherefore, beloved, seeing that ye look for such things, be diligent that ye may be found of him in peace, without spot, and blameless.
>
> And account that the longsuffering of our Lord is salvation; even as our beloved brother Paul also according to the wisdom given unto him hath written unto you;
>
> As also in all his epistles, speaking in them of these things; in which are some things hard to be understood, which they that are unlearned and unstable wrest, as they do also the other scriptures, unto their own destruction.[1]

---

[1]See II Peter 3:14-17.

20

What of the Witch of Endor and Samuel?

Question: *"In the twenty-eighth chapter of First Samuel, the story is related how Saul king of Israel, after the Prophet Samuel died, sought out the witch of Endor to have her 'bring up Samuel,' after that prophet had died, so that he, Saul, could seek advice of him. Now what I have wondered is this: How was it possible for a witch to be able to have power to bring back the spirit of a prophet of God? I know that the devil has great power, but how could he have such power over a prophet of God such as this story seems to indicate? I will be very happy for your help in solving this problem."*

Answer: There are several things incident to this story that the ordinary reader surmises which are not necessarily in harmony with the facts. In the first place Saul did not see the spirit that was called up. All the information that he received was from the statement of the woman herself. No doubt this woman was well acquainted with Samuel and could readily describe him. It is feasible for one to think that the woman was keen enough to realize the situation and the hopelessness of the position of Saul. However, the fact remains that she, it was, who saw and who described the apparition, not Saul.

President Penrose's Summarization Quoted

President Charles W. Penrose in May 1898,[1] wrote an excellent article on this question, and I cannot do better than to repeat it as it gives us a proper summarization of this event:

There are differences of opinion as to the facts narrated in the Bible concerning the visit of Saul, King of Israel, to the Witch of Endor and her purported interview with the spirit of the departed Prophet Samuel. The popular view of this matter is that the witch, at the request of King Saul, "brought up" the spirit of Samuel and that Saul conversed with him and learned from him the fate which awaited him in his coming battle with the Philistines. But the question arises, how could a witch, who under the law of Moses was not to be permitted to live, and with whom consultation was forbidden by the Lord, have power to bring forth at her bidding the spirit of a holy prophet? In answer to this query it has been suggested that the woman was not really a witch, but a prophetess who was in hiding. Why she was under the necessity of concealing her whereabouts is not made to appear. It has been alleged that the "prophetess" theory has been held by persons supposed to understand the question thoroughly. Be that as it may, careful investigation of the history of the event will show that there has been great misunderstanding of the subject. Let us first see what the historian relates:

"And the Philistines gathered themselves together, and came and pitched in Shunem; and Saul gathered all Israel together, and they pitched in Gilboa.

---

[1]The article is reprinted here as it appeared in *The Improvement Era*, Vol. I, May 1898, pp. 495-500.

"And when Saul saw the host of the Philistines, he was afraid, and his heart greatly trembled.

"And when Saul inquired of the Lord, the Lord answered him not, neither by dreams, nor by Urim, nor by prophets.

"Then said Saul unto his servants, Seek me a woman that hath a familiar spirit, that I may go to her, and inquire of her. And his servants said to him, Behold, there is a woman that hath a familiar spirit at Endor.

"And Saul disguised himself, and put on other raiment, and he went, and two men with him, and they came to the woman by night; and he said, I pray thee, divine unto me by the familiar spirit, and bring him up whom I shall name unto thee.

"And the woman said unto him, behold, thou knowest what Saul hath done, how he hath cut off those that have familiar spirits, and the wizards, out of the land; wherefore then layest thou a snare for my life, to cause me to die?

"And Saul sware to her by the Lord, saying, As the Lord liveth, there shall no punishment happen to thee for this thing.

"Then said the woman, Whom shall I bring up unto thee? And he said, Bring me up Samuel.

"And when the woman saw Samuel, she cried with a loud voice; and the woman spake to Saul, saying, Why hast thou deceived me? For thou art Saul.

"And the king said unto her, Be not afraid: for what sawest thou? And the woman said unto Saul, I saw gods ascending out of the earth.

"And he said unto her, What form is he of? And she said, An old man cometh up; and he is covered with a mantle. And Saul perceived that it was Samuel, and he stooped with his face to the ground, and bowed himself.

"And Samuel said to Saul, why hast thou disquieted me, to bring me up? And Saul answered, I am sore distressed; for the Philistines make war against me; and God is departed from me, and answereth me no more, neither by prophets, nor by dreams: therefore I have called thee, that thou mayest make known unto me what I shall do.

"Then said Samuel, Wherefore then dost thou ask of me, seeing the Lord is departed from thee, and is become thine enemy?

"And the Lord hath done to him, as he spake by me: for the Lord hath rent the kingdom out of thine hand, and given it to thy neighbour, even to David:

"Because thou obeyedst not the voice of the Lord, nor executedst his fierce wrath upon Amalek, therefore hath the Lord done this thing unto thee this day.

"Moreover the Lord will also deliver Israel with thee into the hand of the Philistines: and tomorrow shalt thou and thy sons be with me: the Lord also shall deliver the host of Israel into the hand of the Philistines." (I Samuel XXVIII:4-19.)

From the foregoing it is clear that the woman whom Saul visited was one of the class placed under ban, by the commandment of God, because they practiced divination with familiar spirits. Neither prophets nor prophetesses were then banished from the land or held in disrespect. It was only persons condemned by the Mosaic law who had to hide from the effects of its enforcement. Saul had tried every legitimate means to obtain supernatural guidance, but, as he had departed from the Lord, the Lord had departed from him. There was no answer from heaven to his inquiries; there was no word of the Lord by prophets; there was no communication through the Urim and Thummim, there was no manifestation by vision or by dream; there was no whispering of the divine spirit. In his desperation, Saul turned to the opposite power. In that he sinned. He knew that he was violating the law of the Lord. When he was serving God, he "put away those that had familiar spirits and the wizards out of the land," but when he fell into darkness he sought the ways of darkness and sealed his own doom. It is written:

"So Saul died for his transgression, which he committed against the Lord, even against the word of the Lord, which he kept not, and also for asking counsel of one that had a familiar spirit, to inquire of it." (I Chronicles X:13.)

The law of God concerning these forbidden arts was given through the prophet Moses, and forms part of the Mosaic code: As for instance:

"Regard not them that have familiar spirits, neither seek after wizards, to be defiled by them: I am the Lord your God. (Leviticus XIX:31.)

"There shall not be found among you any one that maketh his son or his daughter to pass through the fire, or that useth divination, or an observer of times, or an enchanter, or a witch,

"Or a charmer, or a consulter with familiar spirits, or a wizard, or a necromancer.

"For all that do these things are an abomination unto the Lord: and because of these abominations, the Lord thy God doth drive them out from before thee." (Deuteronomy XVIII:10-12.)

The Witch of Endor, then, instead of being a prophetess of the Lord, was a woman who practiced necromancy; that is, communication or pretended communication with the spirits of the dead; but she was led by a familiar spirit. In other words, she was a spiritual medium, similar to those modern professors of the art, who claim to be under the control of some departed notable, and through him or her to be able to communicate with the dead. It should be observed that in the seance with the king of Israel, Saul did not see Samuel or anybody but the medium or witch. She declared that she saw an old man coming up and that he was covered with a mantle. It was she who told Saul what Samuel was purported to have said. Saul "perceived that it was Samuel" through what the witch stated to him. The conversation that ensued between Samuel and Saul was conducted through the medium. All of this could have taken place entirely without the presence of the prophet Samuel. The woman, under the influence of her familiar spirit, could have given to Saul the message supposed to have come from Samuel, in the same way that messages from the dead are pretended to be given to the living by spiritual mediums of the latter days, who, as in the case under consideration, perform their work at night or under cover of darkness.

It is beyond rational belief that such persons could at any period in ancient or modern times, invoke the spirits of departed servants or handmaidens of the Lord. They are not at the beck and call of witches, wizards, diviners, or necromancers. Pitiable indeed would be the condition of spirits in paradise if they were under any such control. They would not be at rest, nor be able to enjoy that liberty from the troubles and labors of earthly life which is essential to their happiness, but be in a condition of bondage, subject to the will and whims of persons who know not God and whose lives and aims are of the earth, earthy.

Nor is it in accordance with correct doctrine that a prophetess or prophet of the Lord could exercise the power to bring up or bring down the spirits of prophets and saints at will, to hold converse with them on earthly affairs. That is not one of the functions of a prophet or a prophetess. The idea that such things can be done at the behest of men or women in the flesh, ought not to be entertained by any Latter-day Saint. The Lord has said:

"And when they shall say unto you, Seek unto them that have familiar spirits, and unto wizards that peep, and that mutter: should not a people seek unto their God? for the living to hear from the dead?

"To the law and to the testimony: if they speak not according to this word it is because there is no light in them." (Isaiah VIII:19-20; Book of Mormon page 96; verses 19-20.)

It has been suggested that in this instance the Lord sent Samuel in the spirit to communicate with Saul, that he might know of his impending doom; but this view does not seem to harmonize with the statements of the case, made in the scripture which gives the particulars. If the Lord desired to impart this information to Saul, why did he not respond when Saul enquired of him through the legitimate channels of divine communication? Saul had tried them all and failed to obtain an answer. Why should the Lord ignore the means he himself established, and send Samuel, a prophet, to reveal himself to Saul through a forbidden source? Why should he employ one who had a familiar spirit for this purpose, a medium which he had positively condemned by his own law?

"But," it is argued, "the prediction uttered by the spirit which was manifested on that occasion was literally fulfilled. Israel was delivered into the hand of the Philistines, and Saul and his three sons and his armor bearer and the men of his staff were all slain. It was therefore a true prophecy." Admitting that as perfectly correct, the position taken in this article is not in the least weakened. If the witches, wizards, necromancers and familiar spirits, placed under the ban of the law, did not sometimes foretell the truth there would have been no need to warn the people against consulting them. If the devil never told the truth he would not be able to deceive mankind by his falsehoods. The powers of darkness would never prevail without the use of some light. A little truth mixed with plausible error is one of the means by which they lead mankind astray. There is nothing, then, in the history of the interview between Saul and the woman of Endor which, rationally or doctrinally, establishes the opinion that she was a prophetess of the Lord or that Samuel actually appeared on that occasion.

There is no satisfactory evidence that the spirits of the departed communicate with mortals through spiritual mediums or any of the means commonly employed for that purpose. Evil spirits, no doubt, act as "familiars" or as "controls" and either personate the spirits of the dead or reveal things supposed to be known only to them and their living friends, in order to lead away the credulous, but those who place themselves under the influence of those powers of darkness have no means by which they can compel the presence of the spirits of the just or induce disclosures from them to the living. They are above and beyond the art of such individuals, and the mediums themselves are frequently the dupes of evil spirits and are thus "deceivers and being deceived."

"My house is a house of order, saith the Lord, and not a house of confusion." When God has anything to reveal, it will come in the way, by the means and through the persons whom he has appointed. If the living desire to hear from the dead they should seek to the Lord, and not to those who presume to rush in "where angels fear to tread." The earthly sphere and the sphere of departed spirits are distinct from each other, and a veil is wisely drawn between them. As the living are not, in their normal condition, able to see and converse with the dead, so, it is rational to believe, the inhabitants of the spiritual domain are, in their normal condition, shut out from intercourse with men in the flesh. By permission of the Lord, persons on either side of the veil may be manifest to those on the other, but this will certainly be by law and according to the order which God has established. By observing that law and refraining from association with persons and influences that know not God and obey not his gospel, the Latter-day Saints will save themselves from subtle deception and much sorrow, and will be more susceptible to the light and inspiration and revelations that proceed from the Eternal Father!

21

How Can First Nephi 3:7 and Doctrine and Covenants 84:4 Be Reconciled?

Question: *"How can we reconcile 1 Nephi chapter 3 verse 7, in which Nephi states that the Lord gives 'no commandments unto the children of men, save he shall prepare a way for them that they may accomplish the thing which he commandeth them,' with Doctrine and Covenants 84:4, wherein the Saints were commanded to build a temple in Independence in that generation, which temple was not built according to the commandment which was given?"*

Answer: There is no conflict whatever in these two passages even if some such contradiction seems to some to be apparent. Usually a generation is considered to be, "The ordinary period of time at which one rank follows another, or from father to son in succession." However when the Savior said to the Jews: ". . . An evil and adulterous generation seeketh after a sign; and there shall no sign be given to it, . . ."[1] he evidently set no definite time limit, but referred to a condition which could prevail indefinitely as long as wickedness endured, though it should extend through several generations from father to son.

[1]Matthew 12:39.

A Reasonable Assumption

It may be reasonable to assume that in giving this revelation to the Prophet the Lord did have in mind the generation of people who would still be living within the one hundred years from the time of the announcement of the revelation, and that they would enjoy the blessings of the temple, and a glorious cloud would rest upon it. It is also reasonable to believe that no soul living in 1832, is still living in mortality on the earth. Notwithstanding this there is nothing in the commandment given to Nephi, neither in his assurance that the Lord would bless him in obtaining the plates that were so essential to the welfare spiritually and temporally of the descendants of Nephi, that in any sense is in conflict with the commandment or promise that was made by the Lord in the revelation given to the Prophet Joseph Smith. We read in another revelation given to the Church in January 1841, where the Lord absolves the members of the Church from the obligation of building the temple, in the following words:

A Revelation from the Lord

Verily, verily, I say unto you, that when I give a commandment to any of the sons of men to do work unto my name, and those sons of men go with all their might and with all they have to perform that work, and cease not their diligence, and their enemies come upon them and hinder them from performing that work, behold, it behooveth me to require that work no more at the hands of those sons of men, but to accept of their offerings.

And the iniquity and transgressions of my holy laws and commandments I will visit upon the heads of those who hinder my work, unto the third and fourth generation, so long as they repent not, and hate me, saith the Lord God.

Therefore, for this cause have I accepted the offerings of those whom I commanded to build up a city and a house unto my name, in Jackson county, Missouri, and were hindered by their enemies, saith the Lord your God.

And I will answer judgment, wrath, and indignation, wailing, and anguish, and gnashing of teeth upon their heads, unto the third and fourth generation, so long as they repent not, and hate me, saith the Lord your God.

And this I make an example unto you, for your consolation concerning all those who have been commanded to do a work and have been hindered by the hands of their enemies, and by oppression, saith the Lord your God.

For I am the Lord your God, and will save all those of your brethren who have been pure in heart, and have been slain in the land of Missouri, saith the Lord.[2]

Sufficient Answer to the Question

This should be a sufficient answer to the question. The Lord accepted at the hands of the members of the Church their efforts and absolved them. It is an interesting thing to know that during the Civil War, that section of Missouri suffered, and the wrath of the Lord was poured out upon it, and some of the people who hindered the work of the Lord partook of this wrath in fulfilment of that prediction.

It should also be remembered that the Lord opened the way for Nephi because the obtaining of the plates was an absolute necessity as Lehi has pointed out. It was a matter of spiritual life or death to have in their possession the sacred records which Nephi was sent back to Jerusalem to obtain. Therefore the Lord overruled all opposition and made it possible for Nephi to accomplish the work assigned to him. Some critics may arise

[2]D. & C. 124:49-54.

and say why then, could not the Lord overrule all opposition in the day of the Prophet Joseph Smith and make it possible for the building of the house of the Lord according to what had been written? It is a sufficient answer to such a question to say, that the real time for the building of that temple had not arrived, therefore the Lord postponed the day. The building of the temple under all the conditions was not an essential requirement in the year 1832. Surely the Lord would have overruled all opposition had there been the necessity at that time for such a magnificent building to be built. To the contrary he absolved the Saints and postponed the day. When considering the word of the Lord concerning the efforts of the members of the Church, it is wrong to think that the members were not diligent in their duties in that day, and that the Lord had been overruled by wicked men, and his commandments had failed.

A Similar Incident of Apparent Failure

A similar incident of apparent failure occurred in the coming forth of the Book of Mormon when through the persistent pleading of Martin Harris the manuscript of the Book of Mormon was permitted to be taken to exhibit to Mrs. Harris and some of her friends. The manuscript was stolen and no doubt those who stole it made changes in it as the Lord indicated that they would. The Prophet and Martin Harris felt that irreparable error had been done, and they at first wondered why the Lord would permit such a serious thing to happen. The truth is that the Lord knew what would happen from the very beginning and had made provision for such a serious blunder. The loss of this manuscript was felt to be a great lesson to the Prophet, which lesson perhaps he greatly needed. The result thereof, however, was that the Lord had in store a better account of the same historical events, far richer in detail. The apparent evil therefore turned out to be a blessing for all who read the Book of Mormon. Surely the Lord knows the end from the beginning, and no matter what the actions of men may be the purposes of the Lord will prevail.

22

What Is Meant by the Waters above the Firmament?

Question: *"In the Book of Moses, chapter 2, verses seven and eight, it says: 'And I, God, made the firmament and divided the waters, yea, the great waters under the firmament from the waters which are above the firmament, and it was so even as I spake.'*

"'And I, God, called the firmament Heaven; and the evening and the morning were the second day.'

"My question is this: What is meant by the waters above the firmament? None of the members of the class have the answer!"

Answer: The waters above the firmament is a reference to the clouds and the waters which exist in the atmosphere above the earth.

The meaning of the "firmament" as we find it in Genesis, chapter two, verse eight as given in the *Standard Dictionary,* is "The expanse of heaven; the sky." The word "firmament" according to its original meaning connotes something compact, solid, or firm, and at one time there was the belief that the earth was the center of the universe, that the sun, moon, and stars revolved around the earth. However this was not the belief in the beginning. The ancient inhabitants of the earth, from the days of Adam down, for centuries understood that this earth is a *globe,* or a world, revolving in space around the sun. We read in the Book of Moses that the ancient inhabitants of the earth had a perfect understanding in relation to this earth and other earths which the Lord created. We are informed that Methuselah was an astronomer and was well acquainted with the stars. Dr. D. E. E. Hart-Davies, in an article published in the *Journal of Transactions* (Victoria Institute) in discussing this question has this to say:

Comment by Dr. Hart-Davies

But, as a matter of fact, the idea expressed by the English word, "firmament" from the Latin *firmamentum,* which does denote something strong and solid, is not found in the original Hebrew. The word there is (*raqia*), which means that which is stretched out, attenuated, or extended. The verbal form of the root was used to describe the beating-out of gold into thin wires or threads fine enough to be sewn into the priestly garment. The extremely thin gold-leaf which remains after the goldsmith has finished his task represents the *raqia* of the piece of pure metal which he began. The noun, therefore, denotes extension. Hence the R. V. rendering is "expanse" which is correct. The Hebrew is a strictly accurate term. The word, "firmament" is a mistranslation due to the false astronomy of Alexandria in the third century B.C. The Greeks believed that the sky was a solid crystalline sphere. Hence the *raqia* of the Hebrew was rendered in the Greek Septuagint version by the word *steroma,* which was again translated into the Latin Vulgate by *Firmamentum,* from which the A. V. word "Firmament" was derived.

Teachings from the Book of Abraham

We read in the Book of Abraham that the Lord revealed to the ancient worthies many things pertaining to his kingdom, and how he had created worlds without number, and that they have passed through the same course of development that we are going through today and have gone on to their glory. The ancient prophets wrote and sang about the stars. They were well acquainted with them. The shepherds out with their flocks at night sang and wrote about the stars. What is there more beautiful than the words of David that perhaps he sang while tending his flocks in the clear shining of the stars on a beautiful spring evening:

> When I consider thy heavens, the work of thy fingers, the moon and the stars, which thou has ordained;
>
> What is man, that thou art mindful of him? and the son of man, that thou visitest him?
>
> For thou hast made him a little lower than the angels, and hast crowned him with glory and honour.
>
> Thou madest him to have dominion over the works of thy hands; thou hast put all things under his feet: . . .
>
> O Lord our Lord, how excellent is thy name in all the earth[1]

It is a foolish notion to think that the ancient inhabitants of the earth were ignorant of the heavenly bodies. They were acquainted with many of the constellations and the movements of the planets and sang about them. Thus Deborah and Barak, after their victory over the Canaanites sang a song of triumph in which they said: " . . . the stars in their courses fought against Sisera."[2] Moreover, we read in the words of Job, that he was *evidently* an astronomer, at least was well acquainted with the stars: In his defense against the accusations of his tormentors he said:

> I know it is so of a truth: but how should man be just with God?

---

[1]Psalm 8:3-6, 9.
[2]Judges 5:20.

If he will contend with him, he cannot answer him one of a thousand.

Then speaking of the power of the Lord he says:

Which removeth the mountains, and they know not: which overturneth them in his anger.

Which shaketh the earth out of her place, and the pillars thereof tremble.

Which commandeth the sun, and it riseth not; and sealeth up the stars.

Which alone spreadeth out the heavens, and treadeth upon the waves of the sea.

Which maketh Arcturus, Orion, and Pleiades, and the chambers of the south.

Which doeth great things past finding out; yea, and wonders without number.[3]

Ancient Peoples Understood Nature of This Earth

From these passages written anciently we learn that the people of the Lord from the beginning knew the nature of this earth, the course it is pursuing which is the same that has been covered by other worlds throughout the eternities. They were not ignorant of the planets circling our sun in their established courses.

It was not until a later age, when men had fully departed from the teachings of the prophets, that mankind lost touch with the heavens and began to look upon the earth as the great center around which everything revolved. It was at this period of time when the word *firmamentum* was substituted in the writings of Moses. Should we endeavor to change it? The natural answer

[3]Job 9:2-3, 5-10.

to this question is no! We have become so accustomed to speaking of the firmament of heaven that the meaning of the word when so expressed has a far different connotation from what it did perhaps when the translators first employed it. Today everyone knows what is meant by the firmament of heaven. That it is not a solid dome but the open expanse of heaven.

The question naturally has been asked, why did not Joseph Smith change the word back to its original connotation? Why should he have done so when the whole world had become familiar with the interpretation as the word *firmament* is applied to the expanse of heaven?

Nephites Had Perfect Understanding of the Heavens

In the Book of Mormon we discover that the Nephites had a perfect understanding of the heavens. The Aztec calendar stone, seen in many places in Mexico, is a remarkable manifestation of the wisdom and scientific knowledge of the ancient inhabitants of the American continent. They were not ignorant people when they were keeping the commandments of the Lord, and they understood the heavens as well as people do today.

Even my days go back to the time when the astronomers were speaking of the great galaxies scattered throughout the universe as great masses of cloud dust out of which worlds are created. Today with their more nearly perfect methods and instruments for discovery and measurement they have now come to the truth which the Lord revealed to Moses, that these great clusters—galaxies—of stars are separate and distinct universes; moreover, that space is filled with them—some of them so far away from us that it has taken hundreds, yes, in some cases thousands of light years for the light which reaches us to come to us from these wonderful galaxies. What a great and wonderful thing this is! It all confirms the words of the Lord to Moses:

> . . . The heavens, they are many, and they cannot be numbered unto man; but they are numbered unto me, for they are mine.
>
> And as one earth shall pass away, and the heavens thereof even so shall another come; and there is no end to my works, neither to my words.
>
> For behold, this is my work and my glory—to bring to pass the immortality and eternal life of man.[4]

---

[4]Moses 1:37-39.

23

"... All That Are in Their Graves Shall Hear His Voice"

Question: *"There are those who teach that the wicked shall be annihilated at death—the destruction of the spirit as well as of the body. Others teach that the spirit sleeps. What assurance is there that the dead shall hear the voice of God?"*

Answer: The following quotation from the words of the Savior as recorded in the Gospel of John give answer to the question:

Verily, verily, I say unto you, The hour is coming, and now is, when the dead shall hear the voice of the Son of God: and they that hear shall live.

For as the Father hath life in himself; so hath he given to the Son to have life in himself;

And hath given him authority to execute judgment also, because he is the Son of man.

Marvel not at this: for the hour is coming, in the which all that are in the graves shall hear his voice,

And shall come forth; they that have done good, unto the resurrection of life; and they that have done evil, unto the resurrection of damnation.[1]

The resurrection must be just as universal as was the

---

[1]John 5:25-29.

fall. Therefore it embraces everything on the earth and the earth itself, for the earth partook of the changed condition after the transgression of Adam and Eve. Not only was the earth changed, but the same condition of mortality also came upon every living creature. Therefore there must be a restoration not only of Adam and Eve and their posterity, but also of the earth itself and all living creatures on its face.

We have received witnesses of the fulfilment in part at least of the predictions made by Jesus to his disciples in relation to the restoration of all things. At the time of the coming forth of Jesus from the tomb, there followed a resurrection, and Matthew speaking of this has written:

> And the graves were opened; and many bodies of the saints which slept arose,
>
> And came out of the graves after his resurrection, and went into the holy city, and appeared unto many.[2]

There Is No Excuse for Doubt

Why should any person doubt the truth of the universal resurrection? That our Savior lived, that he died on the cross and arose on the third day is attested by divine witnesses. The writings of Matthew, John, and Peter in relation to the resurrection bearing witness is, or should be, beyond dispute. It is the duty and privilege of every member of the Church to have a divine testimony of this great truth. We know, for the witness is before us in definite and positive testimony from the Prophet Joseph Smith, Oliver Cowdery, and others, who in this dispensation have stood in the divine presence

---

[2]Matthew 27:52-53.

of the Son of God! It is, moreover, the duty of every faithful member of the Church to know for himself through the power of the Holy Ghost which is given him that Jesus lives, that he died and is alive again clothed with glory and majesty and that he rules with his Father in the heavens.

The Blessing of Resurrection Is for All Creatures

We also know, because the Lord has revealed it, that through the love of our Redeemer not only those who believe in him and keep his commandments shall come forth from the grave, but this great blessing has been bestowed on all, not only the righteous, but that it will come to every living creature also. Justice demands that there shall be this universal restoration. Jacob, brother of Nephi, has declared this great truth by the spirit of revelation in the following words:

> For as death hath passed upon all men, to fulfil the merciful plan of the great Creator, there must needs be a power of resurrection, and the resurrection must needs come unto man by reason of the fall; and the fall came by reason of transgression; and because man became fallen they were cut off from the presence of the Lord.
>
> Wherefore, it must needs be an infinite atonement—save it should be an infinite atonement this corruption could not put on incorruption. Wherefore, the first judgment which came upon man must needs have remained to an endless duration. And if so, this flesh must have laid down to rot and to crumble to its mother earth, to rise no more.[3]

We therefore have the assurance that the resurrection shall reach out and embrace every creature, even the earth itself. For this earth must be cleansed from

[3] II Nephi 9:6-7.

all unrighteousness and be crowned with glory and eternal life.

To the Prophet Joseph Smith the Lord gave this glorious revelation:

A Glorious Revelation

And again, verily, verily, I say unto you that when the thousand years are ended, and men again begin to deny their God, then will I spare the earth but for a little season;

And the end shall come, and the heaven and the earth shall be consumed and pass away, and there shall be a new heaven and a new earth.

For all old things shall pass away, and all things shall become new, even the heaven and the earth, and all the fulness thereof, both men and beasts, the fowls of the air, and the fishes of the sea;

And not one hair, neither mote, shall be lost, for it is the workmanship of mine hand.

But, behold, verily I say unto you, before the earth shall pass away, Michael, mine archangel, shall sound his trump, and then shall all the dead awake, for their graves shall be opened, and they shall come forth—yea, even all.

And the righteous shall be gathered on my right hand unto eternal life; and the wicked on my left hand will I be ashamed to own before the Father;

Wherefore I will say unto them—Depart from me, ye cursed, into everlasting fire, prepared for the devil and his angels.

And now, behold, I say unto you, never at any time have I declared from mine own mouth that they should return, for where I am they cannot come, for they have no power.

But remember that all my judgments are not given unto men; and as the words have gone forth out of my mouth even so shall thev be fulfilled, that the first shall be last, and that the last shall be first in all things whatsoever I have created by the word of my power, which is the power of my Spirit.[4]

---

[4]D. & C. 29:22-30.

24

Intelligences and Eternal Life

Question: *"Within the Church we are taught that there was life before mortality and that there will be a life hereafter. Also that before we were spirits we were 'intelligences.' The scriptures declare that we are also 'begotten sons and daughters unto God in the spirit (D. & C. 76:24), and Paul speaking to the Greeks declared that we are the 'offspring of God' and ought not to think of the Godhead as gold, silver, or stone graven by the art of man's device. We are also told that 'intelligences' have always existed and can neither be created nor destroyed. Moreover in the Pearl of Great Price, in the Book of Moses, it states that God created animals and all life here on the earth for the purpose of man, and it is for this life only. This has bothered me, for while 'intelligences' were neither made nor created and therefore cannot be destroyed, I have wondered why animals were created for this life only. Is not the difference between man and animals a matter of degree of intelligence, just as the difference between man and God is? Why then should animals be for this life only?"*

Answer: First let us consider the question of intelligences. There are many things that the Lord, for a wise purpose, has not revealed to mortal man, evidently because in mortality man is unable to comprehend them. In *The Progress of Man,* by Joseph Fielding Smith, page eleven, the following is quoted:

"Man Was Also in the Beginning with God"

"Man was also in the beginning with God. Intelligence, or the light of truth, was not created nor made, neither indeed can be. . . . For man is spirit. The elements are eternal, and spirit and element, inseperably connected, receive a fulness of joy; and when separated, man cannot receive a fulness of joy." [D. & C. 93:29, 33-34.]

Some of our writers have endeavored to explain what an intelligence is, but to do so is futile, for we have never been given any insight into this matter beyond what the Lord has fragmentarily revealed. We know, however, that there is something called intelligence which always existed. It is the real eternal part of man, which was not created nor made. This intelligence combined with the spirit constitutes a spiritual identity or individual.

There are so many things in the gospel which are essential for us to know and observe, that we need not bother about the mysteries which have never been revealed. There are many things that we will know when we receive the resurrection and attain to the glories of the kingdom of our Eternal Father, which we cannot understand in this mortal state even if they were revealed to us. The Lord expects us to spend our time preparing for eternity, and he has given us his laws and will reveal to us line on line as we study, all things that are essential for our preparation for salvation in his celestial kingdom. It is the duty of the children of men to seek out fundamental truths and ordinances of the gospel which are made known. A little child commences its motivation by creeping on the floor. Then a step or two holding on to a chair or other object, and eventually it gains power and confidence to move short distances to the waiting hands of its mother. Thus step by step it becomes strong. We may be compared to this little child. We gain knowledge, wisdom, and power to act by observation, study, and practice of correct principles. Too many members of the Church expect the Lord to make known to them his purposes, to reveal knowledge, to give them wisdom, without their putting forth any physical, mental, or prayerful effort. Knowledge, like anything else worthwhile, comes to the individual through his study and practice. The words of Alma declared to Zeezrom should be an incentive to every seeker after truth. It is as follows:

Alma's Words to Zeezrom

> It is given unto many to know the mysteries of God; nevertheless they are laid under a strict command that they shall not impart only according to the portion of his word which he doth grant unto the children of men, according to the heed and diligence which they give unto him.
>
> And therefore, he that will harden his heart, the same receiveth the lesser portion of the word; and he that will not harden his heart, to him is given the greater portion of the word, until it is given unto him to know the mysteries of God until he know them in full.
>
> And they that will harden their hearts, to them is given the lesser portion of the word until they know nothing concerning his mysteries; and then they are taken captive by the devil, and led by his will down to destruction. Now this is what is meant by the chains of hell.[1]

Every Living Thing Entitled to a Resurrection

Now, as to the second question:

A careful reading of the first chapter of Genesis, and the third chapter of Moses in the Pearl of Great Price, will show that the animals were all created and

[1]Alma 12:9-11.

placed on the earth preceding the coming of Adam and Eve. In fact the whole earth and the creatures on it were prepared for Adam and Eve before Adam's fall. In that condition the earth and all upon it were not subject to death until Adam fell. When Adam and Eve partook of the fruit of the tree of knowledge of good and evil, the same judgment was placed on the earth and all things upon it. Therefore every living thing, including the earth itself, partook of the same condition of mortality. Therefore every living thing, including the earth itself, is entitled to death and the resurrection. There is nothing in the Book of Moses that in any way indicates a condition to the contrary.

We read in the Book of Moses the following:

> And now, behold, I say unto you, that these are the generations of the heaven and of the earth, when they were created, in the day that I, the Lord God, made the heaven and the earth;
>
> And every plant of the field before it was in the earth, and every herb of the field before it grew. For I, the Lord God, created all things, of which I have spoken, spiritually, before they were naturally upon the face of the earth. For I, the Lord God, had not caused it to rain upon the face of the earth. And I, the Lord God, had created all the children of men; and not yet a man to till the ground; for in heaven created I them; and there was not yet flesh upon the earth, neither in the water, neither in the air.[2]

In the ninth verse of this same chapter the Lord declares:

> And out of the ground made I, the Lord God, to grow every tree, naturally, that is pleasant to the sight of man; and man could behold it. And it became also a living soul. For it was spiritual in the day that I created it; for it remaineth in the

---

[2]Moses 3:4-5.

sphere in which I, God, created it, yea, even all things which I prepared for the use of man; and man saw that it was good for food. And I, the Lord God, planted the tree of life also in the midst of the garden, and also the tree of knowledge of good and evil.[3]

Answers Presented from Doctrine and Covenants

Since all creatures and the plants and trees of the earth were created spiritually, we discover that not only man is entitled to the resurrection but every other living thing that suffered the fall through Adam's transgression. We read in the Doctrine and Covenants, Section 77, the following in answer to a question put to the Prophet Joseph Smith:

Q. What are we to understand by the four beasts, spoken of in the same verse [Rev. 4:6]?

A. They are figurative expressions, used by the Revelator, John, in describing heaven, the paradise of God, the happiness of man, and of beasts, and of creeping things, and of the fowls of the air; that which is spiritual being in the likeness of that which is temporal; and that which is temporal in the likeness of that which is spiritual; the spirit of man in the likeness of his person, as also the spirit of the beast, and every other creature which God has created.[4]

Also in Section 29, verses 22-26 in the Doctrine and Covenants, we find the following:

And again, verily, verily, I say unto you that when the thousand years are ended, and men again begin to deny their God, then will I spare the earth but for a little season;

And the end shall come, and the heaven and the earth shall be consumed and pass away, and there shall be a new heaven and a new earth.

---

[3]*Ibid.*, 3:9.
[4]D. & C. 77:2.

For all old things shall pass away, and all things shall become new, even the heaven and the earth, and all the fulness thereof, both men and beasts, the fowls of the air, and the fishes of the sea;

And not one hair, neither mote, shall be lost, for it is the workmanship of mine hand.

But, behold, verily I say unto you, before the earth shall pass away, Michael, mine archangel, shall sound his trump, and then shall all the dead awake, for their graves shall be opened, and they shall come forth—yea, even all.[5]

So we learn that this mortal earth, like all on its face, is growing old, and eventually shall die, be cleansed, and then come forth a celestial world and everything will be restored to life never to die again. This does not mean, however, that everything that has been on this earth in mortality will be assigned to remain on this earth when it is purified and has received the celestial glory and becomes a fit abode for celestial beings, human, animal, and plant, according to the divine decree.

---

[5] *Ibid.*, 29:22-26.

25

Is Euthanasia, or Mercy Killing, Ever Justifiable?

Question: *"In our study class the question was raised whether or not there was ever a time when mercy killing would be justifiable? For instance here is an elderly person very ill with a disease which the doctors state cannot be cured. The doctor states that he can prolong the life and thus continue the suffering, but death inevitably would finally result. Would he be justified in taking steps to hasten death and end the physical torment of the patient? If consent was given for the doctor to take such a step to hasten death, would he and those who sanctioned it be guilty and have to answer at the time of the judgment?"*

Answer: The answer to this question is a simple one. The taking of life was condemned when Cain slew Abel, and for his dreadful sin Cain was punished far worse than to have been put to death. After Noah and his family came out of the ark, the Lord renewed this commandment and said:

> Whoso sheddeth man's blood, by man shall his blood be shed: for in the image of God made he man.[1]

---

[1]Genesis 9:6.

Who Has the Wisdom to Make Decision?

Who has the wisdom to say that in case of extreme sickness and suffering, there is ever a time when the hope of recovery is past? There have been cases reported many times of persons who were apparently at the point of death and who were in severe pain, who eventually recovered. The answer to this question in brief is, that to presume that the time has come when the person who is ill cannot recover and it would be justifiable to end the suffering by a painless death is a presumptuous conclusion. The commandment given to Noah is still in force and will be a part of the divine law as long as mortality endures.

This question of "mercy" killing, or euthanasia, constantly arises in the case of individuals who are in severe pain and afflicted with apparently no hope of recovery. It has also been considered in the case of children who are afflicted with some serious deformity which would make them a burden not only to themselves but also to others all the days of their lives. However, there is the matter of conscience which would haunt those who were guilty so that they would live with a feeling of having committed an offense which is unforgiveable, and it seems that they would have no peace.

The discussions on this question apparently will never cease. In the year 1936, this question of "mercy" deaths was presented in a bill before the British House of Lords. This bill was for the purpose of permitting science to decide whether persons should be granted their desire for painless death and was introduced by Lord Ponsonby, Labor leader. Commenting on this *The Deseret News* gave the following:

Comment from The Deseret News

In England as in other countries, recent years have seen a growing movement to legalize "mercy killings" for incurables. Great Britain's several "mercy trials" have served to arouse interest in the movement, and for more than a year the Euthanasia Legalization Society, supported by prominent physicians and church leaders, has been campaigning for what is termed "easy death" in certain cases.

Since an English doctor confessed to taking the lives of five "incurables," doctors and laymen have been debating the right and wrong of ending the suffering of people who are doomed to life-long torture and do not wish to live.

According to the terms of the bill, under debate in the British Parliament, the law would be operated under a referee, who would be appointed by the Minister of Health. Permission of the referee would be necessary before a life could be taken. The act would be restricted specifically to "illness involving severe pain or an incurable and fatal character."

The petitioner for "mercy death" would have to be over 21 years of age, and of sound mind. His application would have to be in his own writing and witnessed by two physicians. If granted, the proposed "easy death" might be administered only by a specially licensed physician in the presence of an official witness.

It appears that civilization has already answered this question without having realized it. The common conscience of mankind declares it a sin and a crime for any private person to take the life of another. But it also recognizes that the law, whether it be the will of the king or the will of the people, is the only human agency that has the right to take the life of a human being.

Killing by the state, by an officer of the law, or by a soldier in battle is the only killing now considered justifiable and not wrong. Therefore, homicide is blameless if sanctioned by law. But we still face the Sinai law—Thou Shalt Not Kill—which in its broad interpretation would place a ban upon any taking of human life.

While this discussion was going on in relation to the question of euthanasia in Great Britain, the Salt Lake *Tribune* also joined in condemnation of such a principle and the following is taken from an editorial in that paper of March 12, 1935:

Comment from The Salt Lake Tribune

The taboo against murder is so strong and deep-seated in our culture that the question of its rightness or wrongness seldom comes up for consideration. Unlike the more controversial issues upon which public sentiment is more or less evenly divided, the universal belief in the justifiability of murder tends to keep the subject beyond the realm of controversy.

When border-line cases arise, however, it becomes not only a matter of news; it is also the occasion of the grounds for our belief. Much publicity has, therefore, attached to the case of the 62-year-old woman in England who deliberately put her imbecile son "to sleep." The woman was tried, convicted, and sentenced to hang for the murder of her invalid son, whom she had nursed for 30 years. In response to the widespread demand of the British public, the home secretary, however, recently reprieved the woman.

Many people will justify the act of the well-intentioned old lady on the ground that the painless extermination of a helpless defective is a justifiable, nay humane, act. Such an argument, however, loses sight entirely of the social consequences involved. Under such a precedent, anyone, not merely a parent, might assume the right to decide that a given person—not alone a defective—would be better off dead. In a spirit of vengeance, or with a paranoid belief in his own superior judgment, a person might thus administer a death potion entirely without authority and wholly without justification.

In a civilization that has achieved a measure of success in compensating for many of nature's deficiencies, and in a society that has only just learned the art of prolonging life, it seems a bit premature to encourage the practice of deliberate killing. Moreover, the question of whether a specific disease or a given defect is incurable is not easy to decide; for it is not always a matter of fact. Even with our present limited knowledge of endocrinology, for instance, many imbeciles such as the one Mrs. Brownhill mercifully put "to sleep" might be cured, provided, of course, the deficiency is not an inherited one. Many conditions which a few years ago were regarded as incurable are now turning out to be within the range of improvement, if not a cure. Until the discovery of insulin, for instance, diabetes was considered hopeless. Pernicious anemia was, until very recently, likewise regarded fatal. The prognosis for general paralysis of the insane, was everywhere considered poor until an Austrian psychiatrist discovered a treatment which has made it one of the most hopeful of all the various forms of insanity.

There are cases, we admit, in which it would seem humane to painlessly exterminate a futile life. But the practical question is, "who shall say?" Public sentiment is apparently not yet ready to allow even a well-trained, high-minded physician to exercise this discretion on such a point.

Given our limited knowledge and the frailty of human nature it would seem, therefore, that the lives of a few hopeless defectives are not to be weighed against the possible subversive consequences of allowing a parent, or even a "board of exterminators" to decide such issues of life and death.

The Life of Every Person Is in the Hands of the Lord

Let us remember that the life of every person is in the hands of the Lord. Mortal man has not been given the right to judge whether or not a defective soul should remain or be taken from this mortal life. Neither is it within our province to say when a person has completed his mortal course. No other person ever suffered as intensely as did the Son of God, which suffering, as he said, " . . . caused myself, even God, the greatest of all, to tremble because of pain, and to bleed at every pore, and to suffer both body and spirit—and would that I might not drink the bitter cup, and shrink—

"Nevertheless, glory be to the Father, and I partook and finished my preparations unto the children of men."[2]

We must come to the conclusion, after a careful consideration of this question, that the conscience of any normal person would trouble that person all the days of mortal life, if guilty of such an act. As far as suffering any penalty is concerned that would be a matter deferred to the final judgment.

---

[2]D. & C. 19:18-19.

26

Who Were the Prophets Zenos and Zenock?

Question: *"In our study of the Book of Mormon and the Book of Moses, it seems to us that Zenos and Zenock, spoken of in the Book of Mormon could have been Enos, the third from Adam, and Enoch, the son of Jared and father of Methuselah. The Bible states, however, that Enoch was translated rather than to have been stoned to death. How else could the Nephites be a remnant of their seed? This may not be important, but we would like the matter cleared for the benefit of our thinking."*

Answer: Outside of what is written in the Book of Mormon, we have no record of either of these ancient prophets. Therefore there is no stated time as to when they lived. The fact is, however, that there were many prophets in Israel and even before the time of Israel whose records we have not obtained. These two prophets lived sometime preceding the coming of Lehi and his family from Jerusalem. Their writings must have been recorded on the plates which Nephi secured from Laban. They proved to be of great worth to the children of Lehi, having contained a great deal of information concerning the future destiny of Israel.

PROPHETS OF OLD TESTAMENT TIMES

Elder George Reynolds, who was one of the most careful and thorough students of the Book of Mormon, has given us this information in his book, *A Dictionary of the Book of Mormon*:

Zenoch or Zenock. A prophet of Israel, of whose personal history, or to what age he belonged, we know nothing. His writings were familiar to the Nephites, as he is quoted by Nephi (I Nephi 19:10), Alma (Alma 33:15), Amulek (Alma 34:7), Nephi (Helaman 8:20), and Mormon (III Nephi 10:16).

Zenos. A Hebrew prophet, often quoted by the Nephite servants of God. All we are told of his personal history is that he was slain because he testified boldly of what God revealed to him. That he was a man greatly blessed of the Lord with the spirit of prophecy is shown by that wonderful and almost incomparable parable of the vineyard given at length by Jacob (Jacob 5). His prophecies are also quoted by Nephi (I Nephi 19:10, 12, 16), Alma (Alma 33:3, 13, 15), Amulek (Alma 34:7), Samuel, the Lamanite (Helaman 15:11), and Mormon (III Nephi 10:16).[1]

THE LESSER PART OF THINGS JESUS TAUGHT

When the Savior visited the Nephites, he permitted them to receive only the lesser things which he taught the people and withheld the greater things because he knew that the people of that generation were not sufficiently humble and obedient and therefore not ready to receive and abide in the covenants. These are Mormon's words:

And these things have I written, which are a lesser part of the things which he taught the people; and I have written them to the intent that they may be brought again unto this people,

[1]*A Dictionary of the Book of Mormon*, 1954 ed., p. 272.

from the Gentiles, according to the words which Jesus hath spoken.

And when they shall have received this, which is expedient that they should have first, to try their faith, and if it shall so be that they shall believe these things then shall the greater things be made manifest unto them.

And if it so be that they will not believe these things, then shall the greater things be withheld from them, unto their condemnation.

Behold, I was about to write them, all which were engraven upon the plates of Nephi, but the Lord forbade it, saying: I will try the faith of my people.

Therefore I, Mormon, do write the things which have been commanded me of the Lord. And now I, Mormon, make an end of my sayings, and proceed to write the things which have been commanded me.[2]

Again the Lord revealed to Mormon the following significant edict because he knew the frailty and disobedience of the children of men, and even members of the Church who would live in these latter days:

For the Lord said unto me: They shall not go forth unto the Gentiles until the day that they shall repent of their iniquity, and become clean before the Lord.

And in that day that they shall exercise faith in me, saith the Lord, even as the brother of Jared did, that they may become sanctified in me, then will I manifest unto them the things which the brother of Jared saw, even to the unfolding unto them all my revelations, saith Jesus Christ, the Son of God, the Father of the heavens and of the earth, and all things that in them are.

And he that will contend against the word of the Lord, let him be accursed; and he that shall deny these things, let him be accursed; for unto them will I show no greater things, saith Jesus Christ; for I am he who speaketh.[3]

---

[2]III Nephi 26:8-12.
[3]Ether 4:6-8.

Indifference Is a Sad Reflection

What a sad reflection it is that the Lord, knowing the end from the beginning, predicted that even after the Book of Mormon was published and presented to the world, many of those who had entered into covenant with him in the waters of baptism would think so little of the Book of Mormon, that they would pay no heed to its teachings, and by their indifference and lack of faith, the great blessings which the Lord has in store for the faithful have to be withheld because there is so much lack of faith and obedience among his people.

The parable of Zenos, recorded by Jacob in chapter five of his book, is one of the greatest parables ever recorded. This parable in and of itself stamps the Book of Mormon with convincing truth. No mortal man, without the inspiration of the Lord, could have written such a parable. It is a pity that too many of those who read the Book of Mormon pass over and slight the truths which it conveys in relation to the history, scattering, and final gathering of Israel. Such members of the Church unto whom attention has been called to the great significance of this parable have said they fail to comprehend it. It is simple and very clear to the minds of those who earnestly seek to know the truth. No man without divine inspiration could have written such a parable as this.

In brief, it records the history of Israel down through the ages, the scattering of the tribes to all parts of the earth; their mingling with, or being grafted in, the wild olive trees, or in other words the mixing of the blood of Israel among the Gentiles by which the great blessings and promises of the Lord to Abraham are fulfilled. After Abraham had been proved even to the extent of being willing to offer Isaac as a sacrifice, the Lord blessed him with the greatest of blessings, and said to him:

> . . . By myself have I sworn, saith the Lord, for because thou hast done this thing, and hast not withheld thy son, thine only son:
>
> That in blessing I will bless thee, and in multiplying I will multiply thy seed as the stars of the heaven, and as the sand which is upon the sea shore; and thy seed shall possess the gate of his enemies;
>
> And in thy seed shall all the nations of the earth be blessed; because thou hast obeyed my voice.[4]

A Remarkable Parable

This remarkable parable portrays how, as branches of the olive tree (Israelites) were carried to all parts of the earth (the Lord's vineyard) and grafted into the wild olive trees (the Gentile nations). Thus they are fulfilling the promise that the Lord had made.

Today Latter-day Saints are going to all parts of the world as servants in the vineyard to gather this fruit and lay it in store for the time of the coming of the Master. This parable is one of the most enlightening and interesting in the Book of Mormon. How can any person read it without feeling the inspiration of this ancient prophet?

---

[4]Genesis 22:16-18.

27

The Eternal Marriage Covenant

Question: *"The doctrine of eternal marriage and marriage by proxy for the dead is a principal teaching of The Church of Jesus Christ of Latter-day Saints, yet it is written in Luke 20:35 that 'they which shall be accounted worthy to obtain that world, and the resurrection from the dead, neither marry, nor are given in marriage.' Is there not reason to believe there is no marriage beyond this world?"*

Answer: One of the most glorious principles of the gospel is the eternal marriage covenant. When the Sadducees came to the Savior and presented the case of a woman who had had seven husbands and asked him which of these husbands she would have in the next world, it was presumably for the purpose of trapping him if they could. The Savior answered them and said:

> . . . The children of this world marry, and are given in marriage:
>
> But they which shall be accounted worthy to obtain that world, and the resurrection from the dead, neither marry, nor are given in marriage:
>
> Neither can they die any more: for they are equal unto the angels; and are the children of God, being the children of the resurrection.[1]

---

[1]Luke 20:34-36.

Doctrine Misunderstood by Christian World

From this answer given to these Sadducees, the Christian world reached the conclusion that there is no marriage beyond this mortal life. Therefore marriages, whether performed by ministers of religion or by officers of the law who are duly authorized, are performed until death separates the contracting husband and wife. This form of marriage, however, was not from the beginning.

In giving instruction to the Pharisees, the Savior set forth a very different doctrine. They came to him and questioned him on divorce. In the answer which he gave to them he taught the doctrine of the eternal marriage covenant.

> And he answered and said unto them, Have ye not read, that he which made them in the beginning made them male and female,
>
> And said, For this cause shall a man leave father and mother, and shall cleave to his wife: and they twain shall be one flesh?
>
> Wherefore they are no more twain, but one flesh. What therefore God hath joined together, let not man put asunder.[2]

Here we have in the words of Jesus the declaration that the marriage covenant is intended to be eternal.

True Doctrine Revealed to Prophet Joseph Smith

This doctrine of the eternal nature of the marriage covenant was revealed to the Prophet Joseph Smith. It is very significant history that has come down to us in relation to the first marriage on this earth. Before there was any mortal death, the Lord declared:

[2]Matthew 19:4-6.

. . . It is not good that the man should be alone; I will make him an help meet for him.[3]

Therefore Eve was given to Adam, and it is clear from this scripture that the intention was that marriage between the man and his wife was to endure forever, for death had not at that time come upon the earth. This thought must have been in the mind of Paul when he declared to the Corinthian Saints:

Nevertheless neither is the man without the woman, neither the woman without the man, in the Lord.[4]

Moreover, Paul when writing to the Ephesian members of the Church wrote as follows:

For this cause I bow my knees unto the Father of our Lord Jesus Christ,

Of whom the whole family in heaven and earth is named, . . .[5]

There is then a family of God in heaven as well as on earth, and who will be the rightful heirs in that family? Naturally it will be composed of those who were married for time and all eternity in the temple of the Lord, for the Lord has written:

Behold, mine house is a house of order, saith the Lord God, and not a house of confusion.

Will I accept of an offering, saith the Lord, that is not made in my name?

Or will I receive at your hands that which I have not appointed?

---

[3]Genesis 2:18.
[4]I Corinthians 11:11.
[5]Ephesians 3:14-15.

And will I appoint unto you, saith the Lord, except it be by law, even as I and my Father ordained unto you, before the world was?

I am the Lord thy God; and I give unto you this commandment—that no man shall come unto the Father but by me or by my word, which is my law, saith the Lord.

And everything that is in the world, whether it be ordained of men, by thrones, or principalities, or powers, or things of name, whatsoever they may be, that are not by me or by my word, saith the Lord, shall be thrown down, and shall not remain after men are dead, neither in nor after the resurrection, saith the Lord your God.[6]

The Blessings of Eternal Increase

Naturally, if men and women, when they marry become members of the family of God, and are entitled to the blessings of eternal increase after the resurrection, the ordinance and covenant of marriage must be by divine authority. The privilege to perform such marriages cannot be promiscuously assumed by any individual or minister. There is but one at a time who holds these divine keys. He has the authority to delegate authority to others to perform marriages for time and for all eternity, and unless this authority is granted, marriages for time and eternity would not be binding beyond this mortal life. Naturally those who wish to marry must subscribe to the laws of the state. No minister or even elder of the Church has the authority to perform marriages and seal for time and all eternity except those who have been duly delegated the authority from the one who holds these divine keys—the President of the Church.

---

[6]D. & C. 132:8-13.

28

What Did Paul Mean by Being Predestinated?

Question: *"During a recent discussion the question arose as to the full meaning of the remark by the Apostle Paul: 'For whom he did foreknow, he also did predestinate to be conformed to the image of his Son, that he might be the firstborn among many brethren.' (Romans 8:29.) And again in Ephesians 1:5, 'Having predestinated us unto the adoption of children by Jesus Christ to himself, according to the good pleasure of his will, . . .'*

"As we stress education so much, it would appear to me that those who lack education or ability are indeed already assigned to a lesser degree of glory because of this, and those who do not have the advanced education of many, and I think of the pioneers in some respects, have already completed their earth life, and thus regardless of their faith and testimony are destined for something less than what they strived for. To have a talent and not be able to use it seems to me sufficient justification for excuse, particularly under the present economic system of the world, and yet it seems unfair that environment or any system should prevent a person from qualifying for the best in the hereafter.

"I fully believe in repentance as an essential part

of life, also forgiveness, but again we are faced with that predestined end because of our actions, whether right or wrong.

"It would appear, if we consider our pre-existence, that our ultimate end was known from the beginning—and I feel this is strengthened by the fact that whilst I personally do not have the learning of a Von Braun, then I am not going to make the grade regardless of my efforts, merely because my mental abilities are not as great as those mentioned.

"I would appreciate your comment on this matter."

Answer: The passages in question are recorded in scripture as follows:

Blessed be the God and Father of our Lord Jesus Christ, who hath blessed us with all spiritual blessings in heavenly places in Christ:

According as he hath chosen us in him before the foundation of the world, that we should be holy and without blame before him in love:

Having predestinated us unto the adoption of children by Jesus Christ to himself, according to the good pleasure of his will.

To the praise of the glory of his grace, wherein he hath made us accepted in the beloved.[1]

For whom he did foreknow, he also did predestinate to be conformed to the image of his Son, that he might be the firstborn among many brethren.

Moreover whom he did predestinate, them he also called:

---

[1]Ephesians 1:3-6.

and whom he called, them he also justified: and whom he justified, them he also glorified.[2]

Gospel of Salvation Is Based on Faithfulness

It is very evident from a thorough study of the gospel and the plan of salvation that a conclusion that those who accepted the Savior were predestined to be saved no matter what the nature of their lives, must be an error. The gospel of salvation based on faithfulness and obedience to the covenants and laws of the gospel is definitely clear in the doctrines of our Lord and his inspired servants. Surely Paul never intended to convey such a thought that in the pre-existence many were destined by divine decree to be saved no matter what the nature of their mortal lives might be. This might have been one of the passages in Paul's teachings which caused Peter to declare that there are in Paul's writings, "some things hard to be understood, which they that are unlearned and unstable, wrest as they do also the other scriptures, into their own destruction."

We learn from a study of the plan of salvation that every soul was given the gift of free agency. It is a divine law—and a very just law. No man should be forced to choose the course which he may take. Salvation can come to each soul in accordance with absolute freedom of the individual to act. There is no compulsion in the kingdom of God. Human beings are not automatons. They have been given their freedom to believe, to serve, or disbelieve and rebel against the commandments of the Lord. Rewards come based on merit. Salvation is a free gift of God, augmented by the atoning blood of his Beloved Son, but the laws of God are based

[2]Romans 8:29-30.

on merit through faithful adherence to the prescribed laws of God. These divine laws have been in existence through the eternities. They have been tried and tested and proved to be just. No man can obtain salvation without a thorough trial of faith and obedience to the principles of eternal truth which have been established from the beginning for the salvation and exaltation of mankind.

No Exceptions in the Beginning

We may be sure that Paul never intended to convey the thought that there had been exceptions made in the very beginning and that some men were destined to be redeemed and saved in the kingdom of God without complying with the terms on which salvation is established.

All of this being true can we not reach some conclusion that would be justifiable in relation to these statements of Paul? Verily, we can! Let us consider these expressions more closely. Is it not the true meaning that those who were faithful in the pre-existence were "predestined" to be "conformed" to the image of his Son? In the very beginning we are taught that man was "formed" in the image of God. This is the definite statement in the Book of Romans. Then we must not lose sight of the fact that the Father knew the faith and integrity of some of the "great ones" who had been rulers in his kingdom before the world was "formed." They had no doubt proved themselves by trial, and their integrity had been shown in the pre-existent state. Therefore it is possible that Paul, knowing this to be the fact, could with positiveness declare that there were some who were "predestined" because God knew them and had the assurance that they would not fall.

We learn something about the integrity of certain souls in the pre-existence. Through the writings of Abraham we have learned much concerning them, and it is possible that the Lord, knowing their integrity, set them apart to his work with the assurance that they would never fall. Such men were Adam, Enoch, Abraham, Moses, and a great many more through the ages down to the Prophet Joseph Smith.

Many Great and Noble Intelligences

Now the Lord had shown unto me, Abraham, the intelligences that were organized before the world was; and among all these there were many of the noble and great ones;

And God saw these souls that they were good, and he stood in the midst of them, and said: These I will make my rulers; for he stood among those that were spirits, and he saw that they were good; and he said unto me: Abraham, thou art one of them; thou wast chosen before thou wast born.

And there stood one among them that was like unto God, and he said unto those who were with him: We will go down, for there is space there, and we will take of these materials, and we will make an earth whereon these may dwell;

And we will prove them herewith, to see if they will do all things whatsover the Lord their God shall command them;

And they who keep their first estate shall be added upon; and they who keep not their first estate shall not have glory in the same kingdom with those who keep their first estate; and they who keep their second estate shall have glory added upon their heads for ever and ever.[3]

The implication here is very clear that all were

[3]Abraham 3:22-26.

capable of keeping their first estate, but that there would be many who would not do so. Therefore they were to receive rewards according to merit. The promise of reward therefore was open to all based on their faithfulness and obedience. Some of them might not be as alert as others, but the same privilege was offered to all. The principal commandments which bring to mankind exaltation in the kingdom of God are obedience to divine law, devotion to principle, and integrity in seeking for light and truth. Therefore the plodder who put forth every effort in faith and obedience was entitled to the same reward as the one who moved forth more readily or skilfully.

Truth Is Something That Can Be Learned

Truth is something that can be learned. It may take one soul a longer time, but integrity and perseverance certainly will be rewarded. The soul who refuses to obey divine law, or who is not willing to be taught, naturally will lose the reward. However, the goal of perfection is open to all, according to the divine plan, who are obedient and willing to learn. Therefore any person who is devoted to the truth and who labors with all his soul to obtain perfection will not be barred. Eternity, as we look upon it, is evidently a very long time. The power to advance in knowledge by those who are faithful and true surely cannot be limited to mortal life. Therefore there is hope for all if they are willing to put forth the effort. It should also be remembered that knowledge will be more readily obtained when we have passed beyond the portals of mortality. Eternity is a very long time according to mortal man's reckoning, and there is no reason to believe that our means of gaining knowledge and wisdom and truth and every other principle of advancement will be retarded when we have passed the restrictions of mortality.

Just what Paul might have had in mind may not be too clearly expressed in the translation that has come to us. That he taught that some men are destined to be damned must be rejected; likewise that some were predestined to be saved without a trial of their faith. Those who rejected the truth and rebelled were cast out with Lucifer because of the great gift of free agency.

Pre-mortal Spirits Entitled to Mortality

We have reason to believe that all who were privileged to come to this mortal world came because they were entitled by pre-mortal qualifications. It is absurd to think that Paul would teach that in the beginning before the earth was formed, some souls were destined to come to earth, receive tabernacles and then be consigned to perdition and some to be saved. Such a doctrine is contrary to all that has been revealed. Therefore we must seek for a better interpretation. It seems that such an interpretation is readily discovered in this passage notwithstanding there may have been a faulty translation. We are therefore bold enough to say that such an interpretation may be given which will be in full accord with the doctrines taught by the Son of God. Therefore the passage in question is repeated here:

> For whom he did foreknow, he also did predestinate to be conformed to the *image* of his Son, that he might be the first born among many brethren.[4]

Does it not appear perfectly clear that those who

---

[4]Romans 8:29. Italics added.

were consigned to come to this earth and pass through mortality, were *predestined* to come in the image and likeness of the Son of God? This at least gives sense to the passage, for it is true. Man is created with a mortal body as a tabernacle for his eternal spirit in the likeness of the Son of God. This was fully decreed in the very beginning. Not that some souls were to have the privilege of coming and receiving bodies of flesh and bones and then be cast off as sons of perdition forever and some to be saved by pre-existing decree.

29

How Could the Melchizedek Priesthood Be Taken Away from Israel?

Question: *"There is some misunderstanding among the members of our class regarding the statement in the Doctrine and Covenants where we read that the Melchizedek Priesthood was taken away from Israel after the departure of Moses, and the House of Israel was left with the Aaronic Priesthood which holds 'the keys of the administering of angels and the preparatory gospel,' and the carnal commandments. (D&C 84:25-26.) What we are troubled about is how could Israel exist with only the Aaronic Priesthood and the law of Moses or carnal commandments? Now if we understand correctly it requires the Melchizedek Priesthood in order to confirm members of the Church. If the statement is correct, then there was no one left to officiate in the bestowal of the Holy Ghost. Yet Peter states, 'For the prophecy came not in old time by the will of man: but holy men of God spake as they were moved by the Holy Ghost.' (2 Peter 1:21.) We were unable to understand how Israel could continue without ministers who could officiate in the ordinances of the gospel in the offices of the Melchizedek Priesthood. Is there a clear statement in relation to this problem?"*

Answer: When the Israelites left the land of Egypt, the Lord offered to give them the full powers of the priesthood if they would obey his commandments and be faithful to their covenants. They did not prove themselves worthy or prepared for such a blessing. Therefore the Lord withdrew the blessings of the Melchizedek Priesthood from male members of the tribes of Israel and left with them the Aaronic Priesthood, and this likewise was confined to the tribe of Levi which tribe officiated in sacrifices for Israel. This is a very interesting story and should prove to be a lesson to modern Israel.

Israel Greatly Blessed

All through the journey of the Israelites in the wilderness, the Lord gave them an abundance of blessings and poured out upon them many miracles, showing his kindness and consideration for all of which they manifested ingratitude. Their wanderings reveal a very interesting history which should be a benefit and a lesson to us in our journeyings and responsibilities in this the final dispensation so that we will not bring down upon us the displeasure of the Lord.

All through their sojourn in the wilderness, Israel showed the disposition of spoiled children. They evidently failed to comprehend the teachings of the Lord that were given to Moses. Therefore when the time came for Israel to cross the Jordan and enter into their inheritance, the prophetic warning the Lord had given them was fulfilled as recorded in the Book of Numbers.

> And the Lord spake unto Moses and unto Aaron, saying,
>
> How long shall I bear with this evil congregation, which

murmur against me? I have heard the murmurings of the children of Israel, which they murmur against me.

Say unto them, As truly as I live, saith the Lord, as ye have spoken in mine ears, so will I do to you:

Your carcases shall fall in this wilderness; and all that were numbered of you, according to your whole number, from twenty years old and upward, which have murmured against me,

Doubtless ye shall not come into the land, concerning which I sware to make you dwell therein, save Caleb the son of Jephunneh, and Joshua the son of Nun.

But your little ones, which ye said should be a prey, them will I bring in, and they shall know the land which ye have despised.

But as for you, your carcases, they shall fall in this wilderness.

And your children shall wander in the wilderness forty years, and bear your whoredoms, until your carcases be wasted in the wilderness.[1]

Israelites Showed Spirit of Rebellion

Therefore when the time came for the crossing of the Jordan, the adults who had left Egypt had perished, all except two men who had maintained their integrity. Even Moses and Aaron were denied the privilege of entering the promised land.

For forty years the Israelites murmured and showed the spirit of rebellion. They failed to comprehend the great manifestations of the Lord from time to time in their behalf. The Lord blessed them with manna in the wilderness, with quail when they clamored for meat, for springs of water miraculously discovered, and in a thousand ways manifested his love and power in their

---

[1]Numbers 14:26-33.

behalf. Notwithstanding all of this the Lord still loved them and made great promises to them.

When Moses went into the mountain and remained for forty days, they rebelled and turned to the false worship of the Egyptians. On that visit into the mountain the Lord gave to Moses certain commandments written on tables of stone. When Moses discovered the rebellion and idolatry of Israel, he threw down these tables and broke them. What did they contain? Commandments pertaining to the fulness of the gospel!

After this act the Lord called Moses back into the mountain and gave him other commandments on the second tables of stone. Did the second tables contain the same things which were written on the first? *No!* Not in all things! In the Bible translations that are current it is stated that these tables contained the same things which were written on the first, however through the revelation to the Prophet Joseph Smith we have learned that the second tables did not contain all of the things that were on the first. The first contained the authority of the gospel which pertained to the blessings of the Melchizedek Priesthood. Had Israel accepted the first plates in sincere faith, Israel would have had the blessings of the Melchizedek Priesthood and the clear principles of the gospel. The Lord substituted the commandments, and we have them as they are recorded in the Book of Exodus and the blessings of the universal bestowal of the Melchizedek Priesthood were withdrawn.

Information from the Inspired Version

We read in the translation, or inspired revision which was given by divine commandment to the Prophet Joseph Smith concerning the second tables, the following:

And the Lord said unto Moses, Hew these two other tables of stone, like unto the first, and I will write upon them also, the words of the law, according as they were written at the first on the tables which thou brakest; but it shall not be according to the first, for I will take away the priesthood out of their midst; therefore my holy order, and the order, and the ordinances thereof, shall not go before them; for my presence shall not go up in their midst, lest I destroy them.

But I will give unto them the law as at the first, but it shall be after the law of a carnal commandment; for I have sworn in my wrath, that they shall not enter into my presence, into my rest, in the days of their pilgrimage. Therefore do as I have commanded thee, and be ready in the morning, and come up in the morning unto mount Sinai, and present thyself there to me, in the top of the mount.[2]

So we see that Israel through rebellion lost the blessings that were first offered to them. Let it be remembered that it was the intention of the Lord, had Israel been faithful, to give them the fulness of the priesthood. This blessing they could not receive, and therefore they were given the lesser priesthood and the carnal, or temporal law.

Blessings of Holy Priesthood Were Restricted

Let us not lose sight of the fact that all through the history of Israel until the coming of our Redeemer, the blessings of the Holy Priesthood were restricted. It was not given universally to the tribes, but of necessity there had to be some faithful men upon whom the Melchizedek Priesthood was conferred. All of the prophets held the Melchizedek Priesthood, but the Prophet Joseph Smith has informed us that in each case it was by special divine appointment.[3] There was never a time in Israel

---

[2]Exodus 34:1-2. Inspired Version.

[3]*Teachings of the Prophet Joseph Smith*, p. 181.

when there was not a prophet with divine authority with power to confirm and perform other ordinances. We are informed that Elijah was the last of the ancient prophets upon whom the fulness was bestowed. He had power to seal the heavens that it did not rain. He had power to call down fire from heaven, to increase the widow's meal, and to raise the widow's son; the son had died. So other prophets like Isaiah, Jeremiah, Ezekiel, and Daniel were blessed with the Melchizedek Priesthood. They could officiate among the people, but there was no universal bestowal of authority among the tribes, from the time of the entrance of Israel into the promised land, until the coming of our Savior. When he came, the fulness of the gospel and of divine authority was restored.

30

Where Did Alma Get His Authority?

Question: *"Where did Alma get his authority? All we can find is that he received it from God, but there is no detail, and we are left to wonder if it was before he was baptized. We are confused about the whole matter and would appreciate any information you can give us."*

Answer: We should take into consideration in the study of the Book of Mormon the fact that it is an abridgment taken from the records or history that had been kept by the prophets among the Nephites. Therefore, many of the details are lacking. This is equally true of the history of Israel as it has come down through the years to us in the Bible. We are left to accept the fact that Lehi, when he left Jerusalem, held divine authority and that this divine power was handed down from generation to generation until the time of the visitation of the Savior. Moreover, while the detail is lacking, the evidence is very clear that the Melchizedek Priesthood was possessed by the Nephites.

Nephites Did Not Function under Aaronic Priesthood

There were none of the tribe of Levi among them, therefore it was by virtue of the Melchizedek Priesthood that they officiated. There are many passages in the Book of Mormon in which reference is given to the Holy

Priesthood. We should also remember that the record that we have received is an abridgment, and therefore many of the details are of necessity missing. Moreover, we are informed that many important things have been withheld from us because of the hardness of our hearts and our unwillingness, as members of the Church, to abide in the covenants or seek for divine knowledge.

In the case of Alma and his priesthood, we are left to surmise that he legally and divinely received it before the days of King Noah. We read that Zeniff, the father of Noah, was a righteous man. Alma evidently received the priesthood in the days of Zeniff, and at no time did he fully accept the teachings nor with full purpose follow the counsels and procedure of Noah and his wicked priests. It was Alma who was deeply touched at the scathing denunciation of the Prophet Abinadi. Moreover it was Alma who recorded them, for he believed thoroughly in what Abinadi had declared, and he turned from whatever transgression he had committed and set forth with a repentant spirit to gather together all those who were willing to accept the teachings of the martyred prophet. In order to save their lives, Alma and those who followed him were forced to flee into the wilderness.

Elder George Reynolds' Comment

In relation to this, Elder George Reynolds in his valuable work, *Commentary on the Book of Mormon,* Vol. II, has written:

> Alma wrote down all the words he had heard the prophet speak. When Abinadi was condemned to death, Alma became his defender, and thereafter championed his cause. He went

to King Noah and plead for Abinadi's life, that it be spared. We may assume that Alma, from this time forth, kept, or caused to be kept, the records of the Nephites in the Land of Lehi-Nephi; also that he, in like manner, kept the record of the people of the Lord, who were driven into the wilderness by the people of King Noah.

Just at what time Alma received the priesthood is not clearly stated, but we may presume that it occurred before Noah came to the throne. Moreover, we must also conclude that Alma at no time truly entered into the wickedness of this wicked king. To Alma the plea made by the martyred Abinadi pierced his heart, and, believing, he wrote down the words of the martyred prophet and went forth among the people gathering all who were willing to believe. Because of the edict of the king, Alma and his followers were forced to flee to a private and remote spot which they named the "Waters of Mormon." In this secluded place Alma baptized all who truly repented of their sins. The first person baptized was a man named Helam. As Alma baptized Helam he also immersed himself, no doubt feeling the need of repentance, for the spirit of humility was upon him. As he baptized Helam he said:

> . . . Helam, I baptize thee, having authority from the Almighty God, as a testimony that ye have entered into a covenant to serve him until you are dead as to the mortal body; and may the Spirit of the Lord be poured out upon you; and may he grant unto you eternal life, through the redemption of Christ, whom he has prepared from the foundation of the world.
>
> And after Alma had said these words, both Alma and Helam were buried in the water; and they arose and came forth out of the water rejoicing, being filled with the Spirit.[1]

[1]Mosiah 18:13-14.

The question is: Where did Alma get his authority? Evidently he obtained it when he received the priesthood, which through his repentance he had not lost. There can be no serious question in relation to his authority, for it is written:

> And it came to pass that Alma; having authority from God, ordained priests; even one priest to every fifty of their number did he ordain to preach unto them, and to teach them concerning the things pertaining to the kingdom of God.[2]

---

[2]*Ibid.,* 18:18.

31

For Whom Is Vicarious Work Performed?

Question: *"In discussing the question of salvation for the dead the question was asked: 'For whom is vicarious work performed in the temples?' Some of our members thought that this work is to be done for everyone who is dead. Then I read the eighty-fifth section of the Doctrine and Covenants, verses three and four and referred to Ezra 2:62-63, where certain of those returning from Babylon were put from the priesthood. It has been my understanding that vicarious work is for the dead, such as baptism, endowment, etc., for nonmembers of the Church who have passed in death. . . ."*

Answer: The question in Ezra 2:62-63, has nothing to do with the question of salvation of the dead. This passage has reference to those who returned from the captivity who had intermarried among peoples who were not entitled to the blessings of the priesthood. By the action of the authorities these were set aside, and not allowed to participate or take part in the priesthood.

No Baptism for Dead in Days of Ezra

Incidentally, permit me to say, that there was no doctrine taught and no work performed for the dead in the days of Ezra. For that matter there could be no performance of ordinances for the dead in those early times. *Baptism for the dead and the other ordinances pertaining to salvation for the dead were not practiced in Israel or any other place in the world before the resurrection of our Savior.* In fact, it was contrary to the plan of salvation for the ordinances to be performed for the dead until after the Savior had, through his atonement and resurrection, prepared the way for the salvation of the dead. We are taught in the scriptures that this vicarious work was one that had to wait until the power of redemption had been fulfilled in the mission, death, and resurrection of our Lord. It was he who through his atonement on the cross opened the door for the salvation of the dead and made it possible for the living, who held the divine authority by partaking of these glorious gifts themselves in the temples of the Lord, to go into the temples and perform this vicarious work for the dead.

Unfortunately there is very little written in the scriptures that has come down to us that throws any light whatever on the salvation of the dead. That there was established the practice of baptism for the dead in the days following the resurrection of the Savior, we learn from the writings of Paul. However that which is recorded is extremely fragmentary, and we do not gain a clear insight into what was done.

Our Responsibility to Work for the Dead

The doctrine of salvation for the dead was one that evidently had to wait almost entirely for the Dispensation of the Fulness of Times. This work is one of the urgent duties which pertains to the Dispensation of the Fulness of Times, and the Lord has made it obligatory today upon the children to see that the work is done for their fathers. By fathers, we mean the generations of our kindred dead back to the time of Adam.

In an epistle written to the brethren who were in Great Britain in 1840, the Prophet Joseph Smith said:

> I presume the doctrine of "baptism for the dead" has ere this reached your ears, and many have raised some inquiries in your minds respecting the same. I cannot in this letter give you all the information you may desire on the subject; but aside from knowledge independent of the Bible, I would say that it was certainly practiced by the ancient churches; and St. Paul endeavors to prove the doctrine of the resurrection from the same, and says, "Else what shall they do which are baptized for the dead, if the dead rise not at all? Why are they then baptized for the dead?"
>
> I first mentioned the doctrine in public when preaching the funeral sermon of Brother Seymour Brunson: and have since then given general instructions in the Church on the subject. The Saints have the privilege of being baptized for those of their relatives who are dead, who they believe would have embraced the Gospel, if they had been privileged with hearing it, and who have received the Gospel in the spirit, through the instrumentality of those who have been commissioned to preach to them while in prison.[1]

According to the doctrine of salvation for the dead, it is the duty of the children to perform the ordinances for their fathers, in fulfilment of the promise made through the prophets. It was for this purpose that Elijah came to plant in the hearts of the children the promise made by prophecy to the fathers. It is very evident from the revelations and the teachings of the Prophet Joseph Smith, that it is the responsibility of the children to work on the lineage of their fathers and search out their kin-

[1] *DHC* 4, p. 231.

dred dead as far back as they are able to go. Therefore to answer the question, it is our duty to search out our own dead and not labor at random, but endeavor to link generation by generation of our own kindred back from generation to generation as far as we can go.

The Lord's Plan Will Not Fail

If every family in the Church would perform this labor for their dead, they would be doing exactly what the Lord requires of them. If we do our duty, we will find enough to do without overstepping any bounds. We need not worry about what the Lord will do with the numerous dead. We may be sure that his plan will not fail. The work of salvation for the dead will carry on and eventually the work will be performed for every soul who is entitled to receive it. It has been stated with reasonable understanding, that during the millennium and after we have done all that we are able, those on the other side will come to those who are still in mortality and aid in this vicarious work by supplying the necessary information which we are unable to procure. The work of the Lord is perfect, and we should have confidence in him that he will provide the means by which all those who are worthy shall find the means for the ordinances to be granted to them. This, however, does not exempt the living from performing the ordinances for their dead as far as they are able to go.

32

The Church and the Negro

Question: *"Clare Boothe Luce in her 'Without Portfolio' column in the June issue of McCall's Magazine writes an answer to the question: 'Do you think George Romney has a chance of getting the Republican nomination for the presidency in 1964?' And I quote: 'Mr. Romney is a Mormon. It seems that the Mormon Church teaches that the Negroes have inferior souls. If this is so, a Mormon might have some difficulty in carrying the Negro vote in Michigan. But Mr. Romney's own views are known to differ in this respect from those of his church, just as President Kennedy's views on the constitutionality of aid to parochial schools differ from those of the hierarchy of the Roman Catholic Church.'"*

Answer: When uninformed people, speaking of political and other matters, undertake to interpret the position of The Church of Jesus Christ of Latter-day Saints with respect to the status of the Negro, they do the Church a grave injustice and present views which are not correct.

False Premises Lead to False Conclusions

The ignorance on the part of writers who do not belong to The Church of Jesus Christ of Latter-day Saints in relation to the view of the "Mormons" on the status religiously or otherwise of the Negro is inexcusable. There is no doubt that in the campaign, should George Romney become a candidate, enemies will play up the Negro question to the very limit. The pity of it all will be that they start with a false premise and therefore they will naturally end with a false conclusion. The Latter-day Saints, so commonly called "Mormons," have no animosity towards the Negro. Neither have they described him as belonging to an "inferior race." There are Negroes in the Church who are respected and honored for their integrity and faithful devotion. The door into the Church is open to all. One ancient Nephite prophet wrote the following:

> And again, the Lord hath commanded that men should not murder; that they should not lie; that they should not steal; that they should not take the name of the Lord their God in vain; that they should not envy; that they should not have malice; that they should not contend one with another; that they should not commit whoredoms; and that they should do none of these things; for whoso doeth them shall perish.
>
> For none of these iniquities come of the Lord; for he doeth that which is good among the children of men; and he doeth nothing save it be plain unto the children of men; and he inviteth them all to come unto him and partake of his goodness; and he denieth none that come unto him, black and white, bond and free, male and female; and he remembereth the heathen; and all are alike unto God, both Jew and Gentile.[1]

The Church Can Do More for the Negro

Moreover, according to the faith and knowledge of the elders of The Church of Jesus Christ of Latter-day Saints, who are so frequently called "Mormons," the Church can do more for the Negro than any other

[1] II Nephi 26:32-33.

church on the face of the earth. What other church can baptize them by divine authority and confirm them and give them the gift of the Holy Ghost? What other church can promise them with assurance that they can if they are faithful and true before the Lord enter into the celestial kingdom? Not one of them! For other churches do not know anything about the celestial kingdom.

Paul has revealed to the world through the doctrine he taught the Corinthian Saints, that there are three kingdoms, or glories, into which mankind will go. These are the words of Paul:

> All flesh is not the same flesh: but there is one kind of flesh of men, another flesh of beasts, another of fishes, and another of birds.
>
> There are also celestial bodies, and bodies terrestrial: but the glory of the celestial is one, and the glory of the terrestrial is another.
>
> There is one glory of the sun, and another glory of the moon, and another glory of the stars; for one star differeth from another star in glory.
>
> So also is the resurrection of the dead. It is sown in corruption; it is raised in incorruption.[2]

Negroes May Become Heirs of the Celestial Kingdom

Therefore if a Negro joins the Church through the waters of baptism and is confirmed by the laying on of hands and then he remains faithful and true to the teachings of the Church and in keeping the commandments the Lord has given, he will come forth in the first resurrection and will enter the celestial kingdom of God.

What other church can make a better promise?

[2] I Corinthians 15:39-42.

Moreover we know whereof we speak, for the gospel of Jesus Christ has been restored with all its powers and divine authority.

The Negro who accepts the doctrines of the Church and is baptized by an authorized minister of The Church of Jesus Christ of Latter-day Saints is entitled to salvation in the celestial kingdom or the highest heaven spoken of by Paul. It is true that the work of the ministry is given to other peoples and why should the so-called Christian denominations complain? How many Negroes have been placed as ministers over white congregations in the so-called Christian denominations? It appears that a great deal of noise has been made over a problem that does not really exist or is not peculiar to the Latter-day Saints!

Every man whether he seeks office or to maintain a good name in the community should be judged by his devotion and integrity to principles of truth and righteousness, not condemned through rumors, prejudices, or the views of others.

It is strange that so many persons are tried and condemned by well-meaning people because of assumed notions and prejudice without a true knowledge of the facts.

33

The Name of the Church

Question: *"Being a convert to the Church of five years there are perhaps a few things that are more noticeable to me than a person who has grown up as a member. One thing I have found throughout the Church almost without exception is the constant use of the nickname 'Mormons,' in preference to the name given by the Lord whereby his Church should be known: The Church of Jesus Christ of Latter-day Saints. (Doctrine and Covenants 115:4.)*

"Many members of the Church persistently use the name 'Mormon.' When I ask why they do not use the correct name or say that they are Latter-day Saints when speaking to nonmembers, they say it takes too long, or that everyone knows that the real name is 'The Church of Jesus Christ of Latter-day Saints.' It just happens, however, that I myself was unaware of the correct name of the Church while I was a nonmember. When I went into the army I was fortunate enough to bunk next to a member. On a chain along with his dog-tags and a picture of the Salt Lake Temple was the inscription, 'The Church of Jesus Christ of Latter-day Saints.' The temple was familiar to me, and so I inquired of the brother about the medallion. For the first time I found out that the 'Mormon Church' really was not the 'Mormon Church' but The Church of Jesus Christ of Latter-day Saints.

"At present I am enjoying service in my second

stake mission. I find the great majority of people I talk to are not aware that we Latter-day Saints believe that Jesus Christ is the name of the Church and that this is his Church. We, as members, by our constant use of the name 'Mormon' are responsible for the general belief of nonmembers, that we are not in any way followers of the Savior.

"In III Nephi, Chapter 27, the Lord tells his disciples that his Church which is built upon his gospel, must bear his name. No wonder people are confused to what we teach and sometimes think that 'Mormons' are not really Christians."

Answer: It is a fact that the term "Mormon" was applied by bitter enemies of the Church in a spirit of derision because of our acceptance of the Book of Mormon. As time advanced the expression became softened and began to be used by friend and foe alike in reference to the name of the Church and its members.

Book of Mormon Bears Record of Jesus Christ

The criticism that is offered that the members of the Church are universally known as "Mormons" and that the Church is the "Mormon Church," comes of course from our belief in and acceptance of the Book of Mormon, which is the greatest and clearest record that we have, bearing testimony to the great mission of Jesus Christ our Lord. Any person who will sincerely read it will be convinced of its truth and be brought nearer to the Son of God than in any other way.

The Nephites believed in Christ; they wrote and

prophesied of him and his mission, and while there is no opprobrium that can justly be attached to one who believes in the Book of Mormon, there is no valid reason why Latter-day Saints should speak of themselves as "Mormons" or of the Church as the "Mormon Church." Missionaries should not be engaged in "selling Mormonism," but in the mission of persuading people to believe in Christ, the Son of God, and of becoming members of *his* Church—The Church of Jesus Christ. The term *Latter-day Saints* is added to the name merely to distinguish us from the former-day Saints.

Mission of Latter-day Saints Is to Preach Gospel

We are living in the latter days—the days when the Lord promised to restore all things. The mission of the Latter-day Saints is to preach the gospel of Jesus Christ as it has been revealed after a long period of apostasy or departure of the peoples of the world from the teachings of our Savior and his disciples. This divine truth has been restored according to the predictions of the ancient prophets and apostles. Joseph Smith was called to stand at the head of the Dispensation of the Fulness of Times, preparatory to the second advent of the Son of God.

While there can be no disgrace nor condemnation in being called "Mormons," and the Church, the "Mormon Church," the fact remains, and this we should all emphasize, that we belong to The Church of Jesus Christ of Latter-day Saints, the name the Lord has given by which we are to be known and called.

34

Jesus Christ Is Both Father and Son

Question: *"Recently a member of another religious organization visited my home and proclaimed that the Book of Mormon contained various errors and changes that did not appear in the original printing. He further claimed that the Book of Mormon taught there is only one God and that Jesus Christ as God is both Father and Son. It was his contention that Christ could not be an Elder Brother and also our Father, as evidenced by the words of Abinadi. What explanation can we offer?"*[1]

Answer: There are some religious organizations who have centered their attack largely upon the Book of Mormon. They go into the homes of members of the Church and point out to them what they consider to be errors or changes or additions to what was given in the first publication.

Now, if anybody has published a book he knows that the first thing that stares him in the face the moment it comes off the press is some glaring error. We have never claimed that in the beginning there were not some errors which the Prophet corrected, but they were very,

---

[1]Answer for this question was delivered as part of President Smith's address at the 132nd semiannual conference of the Church, October 5, 1962.

very few.[2] But, some of these complaints or charges are against certain writings that appear. . . .

The statement of Abinadi and a similar statement occurs in some other places, that Jesus Christ is both Father and Son to us.

> And now Abinadi said unto them: I would that ye should understand that God himself shall come down among the children of men, and shall redeem his people.
>
> And because he dwelleth in flesh he shall be called the Son of God, and having subjected the flesh to the will of the Father, being the Father and the Son—
>
> The Father, because he was conceived by the power of God; and the Son, because of the flesh; thus becoming the Father and Son—
>
> And they are one God, yea the very Eternal Father of heaven and of earth.[3]

What Is a Father?

What's wrong with that scripture? What is a father? *One who begets or gives life.* What did our Savior do? He begot us, or gave us life from death, as clearly set forth by Jacob, the brother of Nephi. If it had not been for the death of our Savior, Jesus Christ, the spirit and body would never have been united again. As Jacob states:

> And our spirits must have become like unto him, and we become devils, angels to a devil, to be shut out from the presence of our God, and to remain with the father of lies, in misery, like unto himself; yea, to that being who beguiled our first

[2]For further explanation on this subject see *Answers to Gospel Questions*, Vol. II, p. 199, Are There Any Vital Changes in the Book of Mormon? See also Volume I, p. 172, Is There a Contradiction between Alma 7:10 and Matthew 2:5-6?

[3]Mosiah 15:1-4.

parents, who transformeth himself nigh unto an angel of light, and stirreth up the children of men unto secret combinations of murder and all manner of secret works of darkness.

O how great the goodness of our God, who prepareth a way for our escape from the grasp of this awful monster; yea, that monster, death and hell, which I call the death of the body, and also the death of the spirit.

And because of the way of deliverance of our God, the Holy One of Israel, this death, of which I have spoken, which is the temporal, shall deliver up its dead; which death is the grave.

And this death of which I have spoken, which is the spiritual death, shall deliver up its dead; which spiritual death is hell; wherefore, death and hell must deliver up their dead, and hell must deliver up its captive spirits, and the grave must deliver up its captive bodies, and the bodies and the spirits of men will be restored one to the other; and it is by the power of the resurrection of the Holy One of Israel.

O how great the plan of our God! For on the other hand, the paradise of God must deliver up the spirits of the righteous, and the grave deliver up the body of the righteous; and the spirit and the body is restored to itself again, and all men become incorruptible, and immortal, and they are living souls, having a perfect knowledge like unto us in the flesh, save it be that our knowledge shall be perfect.[4]

If there had been no redemption from death our spirits would have been taken captive by Satan and we would have become subject to Satan's will forever.

What Did Our Savior Do?

What did our Savior do? He begot us in that sense. He became a father to us because he gave us immortality or eternal life through his death and sacrifice upon the

[4]II Nephi 9:9-13.

cross. I think we have a perfect right to speak of him as Father.

King Mosiah put his people under covenant to take upon them the name of Christ. And this was 124 years before the birth of Christ. I want to read a verse or two from this pledge.

And now, because of the covenant which ye have made ye shall be called the children of Christ, his sons, and his daughters; for behold, this day he hath spiritually begotten you; for ye say that your hearts are changed through faith on his name; therefore, ye are born of him and have become his sons and his daughters.[5]

Is there anything wrong in our calling Jesus Christ our spiritual Father?

And under this head [this wonderful king said] ye are made free and there is no other head whereby ye can be made free. There is no other name given whereby salvation cometh; therefore I would that ye should take upon you the name of Christ, all you that have entered into the covenant with God that ye should be obedient unto the end of your lives.

And it shall come to pass whosoever does this shall be found at the right hand of God, for he shall know the name by which he is called; for he shall be called by the name of Christ.

And now it shall come to pass, that whosoever shall not take upon him the name of Christ must be called by some other name; therefore, he findeth himself on the left hand of God.[6]

Son of God Rightly Called Father

The Son of God has a perfect right to call us his

---

[5]Mosiah 5:7.
[6]*Ibid.*, 5:8-10.

children, spiritually begotten, and we have a perfect right to look on him as our Father who spiritually begot us.

Now if these critics would read carefully the Book of Mormon they would find that when the Savior came and visited the Nephites he told them that he had been sent by his Father. He knelt before them and he prayed to his Father. He taught them to pray to his Father, but that did not lessen in the least our duty and responsibility of looking upon the Son of God as a Father to us because he spiritually begot us.

35

What Is the Meaning of Ecclesiastes Chapter Nine, Verses Four, Five, and Ten?

Question: *"Will you please explain the meaning of Ecclesiastes, chapter nine, verses four, five, and ten, which are as follows:*

" 'For to him that is joined to all the living there is hope: for a living dog is better than a dead lion.

" 'For the living know that they shall die: but the dead know not anything, neither have they any more a reward; for the memory of them is forgotten. . . .

" 'Whatsoever thy hand findeth to do, do it with thy might; for there is no work, nor device, nor knowledge, nor wisdom, in the grave, whither thou goest.' "

Answer: These passages have led some well-meaning people to believe that the mortal body has no spirit. Others believe that the spirit slumbers as well as the body in the grave. How any intelligent person can accept such a belief in the face of so many passages of scripture teaching that the spirit of man is a complete entity which existed before birth, is joined to the body in mortal life, and continues to exist following death, is something very strange and hard to understand. Moreover, we are assured in the scriptures that the spirit and the body will again be united, never to be separated after the resurrection. The Savior made this very clear when he was in his ministry on the earth with his disciples.

The True Meaning

The true meaning of these passages pertains to a simple fact. That fact is that after a person has passed in death he is soon forgotten. The things of this world about him, its business, pleasures, sorrows are not remembered by loved ones and friends. The world goes on about its business; days come and go as do the seasons; and the earth continues its course through the heavens the same as though the dead had never lived. No matter how great or renowned a person may have been, it is but a short time until he is forgotten. No longer does the dead have any word to give, counsel to impart, and things go on in their natural way without him. Therefore when we look at these passages in their true light, we must agree—the dead are soon forgotten.

Death Does Not Terminate Existence

That the spirit of the dead ceases to exist, to endure, to think or act is a fallacy. Death does not terminate existence. It does not prove that the immortal spirit has in any sense ceased to function. Nor does it prove that there is no spirit which inhabited the dead body. Evidently these words accredited to Solomon were written in his later life after he had transgressed the divine commandments. Whatever the case may be when looked at and examined naturally, we must admit that Solomon was right, at least in large measure. We are in no position in mortality to discourse on or properly evaluate the privileges and opportunities given to the spirits of the dead, but we can say with Solomon that when death intervenes, the body is laid away in the grave peacefully and that it knows nothing as to the affairs of a busy world. Therefore when we speak of the mortal body as an entity, we can fully agree, but the living spirit which belongs to that body is very much alive.

We have never been informed just how much the departed spirit is permitted to know and understand concerning conditions as they continue on earth after death. That the spirit still exists as an entity of vitality, we have every assurance, for it was created to be eternal. The death of the mortal body does not bring a death of the spirit. It continues, has vitality, and looks forward to the day of the resurrection. The idea therefore that the spirit is dormant, or that there is not an eternal spirit is false and is discredited in all the revelations that the Lord has given to man since the days of Adam.

The Spirit Is an Entity

There are numerous instances recorded in the scriptures which point definitely to the fact that the spirit is an entity; that it endures after death because it is eternal. The Bible reveals incidents where the departed have appeared as spirits to the living. The story of Saul and the witch of Endor is not a fallacy, but a definite fact, not that Samuel was "called up," but to the fact that there were spirits in existence. The story of the Savior in relation to Lazarus and the rich man is an evidence of this truth. Our Redeemer would not present a story of fiction of such wonderful significance, if it was not based on truth. No thinking person would accuse the Son of God of presenting an imaginary story of such import as the story of Lazarus and the rich man unless the background was based in truth.

If the disciples of the Lord at the time of his appearance after his resurrection had possessed a foolish notion, thinking that when the Lord appeared to them they were seeing a spirit and there are no spirits, the Lord would have told them plainly that there are no spirits. What was it that he did say?

> Behold my hands and my feet, that it is I myself: handle me, and see; for a spirit hath not flesh and bones, as ye see me have.[1]

This statement by our Savior should put an end to all controversy.

---

[1]Luke 24:39.

36

Condition of Mankind in the Resurrection

Question: *"Is a person resurrected to appear at the same age as that to which he or she had attained when the body was laid down? I realize that children who die will be raised as children for there is no growth in the grave, but will some appear to be thirty years old and some eighty or one hundred, in the resurrection?"*

Answer: There is no reason for any person to be concerned as to the appearance of individuals in the resurrection. Death is a purifying process as far as the body is concerned. We have reason to believe that the appearance of old age will disappear and the body will be restored with the full vigor of manhood and womanhood. Children will arise as children, for there is no growth in the grave. Children will continue to grow until they reach the full stature of their spirits. Anything contrary to this would be inconsistent. When our bodies are restored, they will appear to be in the full vigor of manhood and womanhood, for the condition of physical weakness will all be left behind in the grave.

Teachings of Amulek

Amulek, when speaking to the people of Ammonihah, presented this matter of the resurrection in clearness in the following words:

And he [Jesus Christ] shall come into the world to redeem his people; and he shall take upon him the transgressions of those who believe on his name; and these are they that shall have eternal life, and salvation cometh to none else.

Therefore the wicked remain as though there had been no redemption made, except it be the loosing of the bands of death; for behold, the day cometh that all shall rise from the dead and stand before God, and be judged according to their works.

Now, there is a death which is called a temporal death; and the death of Christ shall loose the bands of this temporal death, that all shall be raised from this temporal death.

The spirit and the body shall be reunited again in its perfect form; both limb and joint shall be restored to its proper frame, even as we now are at this time; and we shall be brought to stand before God, knowing even as we know now, and have a bright recollection of all our guilt.

Now, this restoration shall come to all, both old and young, both bond and free, both male and female, both the wicked and the righteous; and even there shall not so much as a hair of their heads be lost; but everything shall be restored to its perfect frame, as it is now, or in the body, and shall be brought and be arraigned before the bar of Christ the Son, and God the Father, and the Holy Spirit, which is one Eternal God, to be judged according to their works, whether they be good or whether they be evil.

Now, behold, I have spoken unto you concerning the death of the mortal body, and also concerning the resurrection of the mortal body. I say unto you that this mortal body is raised to an immortal body, that is from death, even from the first death unto life, that they can die no more; their spirits uniting with their bodies, never to be divided; thus the whole becoming spiritual and immortal, that they can no more see corruption.[1]

---

[1]Alma 11:40-45.

A Very Clear and Informative Statement

This is a very clear and informative statement in relation to the restoration of the spirit to the body through the mercy of our Savior Jesus Christ. This great truth should impress every living soul with the need of obedience to all of the commandments of the Lord and impel us to be true to every covenant and obligation contained in the fulness of the gospel. The fact that every soul shall live again should be an incentive to all to live in strict obedience to the divine will of our Eternal Father. To be banished from his presence and to be a partaker of the punishment which is in store for those who wilfully and knowingly transgress the laws of the Eternal Father, should impress every soul and impress all to live lives of righteousness. While there will come the universal resurrection, there are various times appointed for the coming forth of the dead.

One great resurrection has already come to humanity. This was at the resurrection of the Son of God. There will be other resurrections yet to come, and all will not come forth at the same time, but this subject need not be discussed at this time. The great truth that is here emphasized is the fact that *all* shall come forth eventually. Moreover, that there will be a restoration of the physical body in its proper frame.

President Joseph F. Smith when speaking at the funeral of Sister Rachel Grant, the mother of President Heber J. Grant, had the following to say in relation to deformities in the resurrection:

> Deformity will be removed; defects will be eliminated, and men and women shall attain to the perfection of their spirits, to the perfection that God designed in the beginning. It is his

purpose that men and women, his children, born to become heirs of God, and joint heirs with Jesus Christ, shall be made perfect, physically as well as spiritually, through obedience to the law by which he has provided the means that perfection shall come to all his children. Therefore, I look for the time to come when our dear Brother William C. Staines, whom we all knew so well, and with whom we were familiar for years—I was familiar with him all my life, just as I was familiar with Aunt Rachel here all my life, and do not remember the time when I did not know her—I look for the time when Brother Staines will be restored. He will not remain the crippled and deformed William C. Staines that we knew, but he will be restored to his perfect frame—every limb, every joint, every part of his physical being will be restored to its perfect frame. This is the law and the word of God to us, as it is contained in the revelations that have come to us through the Prophet Joseph Smith. The point in my mind which I desire to speak of particularly is this: When we shall have the privilege to meet our mother, our aunt, our sister, this noble woman whose mortal remains lie here now, but whose immortal spirit has ascended to God from whence she came, when that spirit shall return to take up this tabernacle again, here will be Aunt Rachel in her perfection. . . . Under the law of restoration that God has provided, she will regain her perfection, the perfection of her youth, the perfection of her glory and of her being, until her resurrected body shall assume the exact stature of the spirit that possessed it here in its perfection, and thus we shall see the glorified, redeemed, exalted, perfected Aunt Rachel, mother, sister, saint and daughter of the living God, her identity being unchanged, as a child may grow to manhood or womanhood and still be the same being.[2]

Resurrected Beings to Come Forth in Perfect Frame

Salvation would be incomplete if individuals should arise in the resurrection with all the deformities, weaknesses, and imperfections that are found in so many of the human family in this mortal existence. We have

---

[2]*Gospel Doctrine,* President Joseph F. Smith, pp. 23-24.

every reason to believe that the spirits of mankind and all other creatures were in a perfect form in the spirit world. It would be an awful stretch of the imagination to think that the imperfections found so frequently in mortality were defects which were designed in the creation. Moreover, as the Lord made it clear in relation to the man who was born blind, it was not an immortal condition.

By the great power and faith of the Son of God, he was able to correct deformity, blindness, and give to the deaf the gift of speech, by the word of his power. The question has frequently been asked when a child has been born with some physical defect or deformity, was this a punishment or a condition which was his before he was born? No! All of these ills are ills of the flesh or defects that are due to mortal conditions which may have come upon the body even before birth, but we may be assured that these defects were not conditions which existed in the world of spirits.

It is the will of the Lord that in the restoration of all things there shall come perfection. The physical defects, some of which may have resulted before birth, are defects which are due to some physical and mortal condition and not an inheritance from the spirit world.

37

Purpose for Temples

Question: *"What is the purpose for temples according to Latter-day Saint belief?"*

Answer: According to the doctrines of The Church of Jesus Christ of Latter-day Saints, a temple is a sacred edifice in which ordinances are performed for both the living and the dead.

The people of the Lord through the ages have been builders of temples. It was impossible for Israel while in bondage and while journeying through the wilderness to build a permanent temple. However, in those days after their departure from Egypt, the Lord commanded Moses to build a temporary temple or sacred edifice which they could set up and take down and carry with them. When they were permanently located in Palestine, they were commanded to replace this portable tabernacle or temple with one that would be permanent. This time came in the reign of Solomon, and in it sacred ordinances were performed.

During the years when a temple could not be built, the servants of the Lord went to the mountaintops to communicate with the Lord. It was on the top of a mountain that Enoch spoke with the Lord. It was on the mountain that Moses did likewise, as did Nephi and the Brother of Jared. When the Latter-day Saints came to the Salt Lake Valley, they performed ordinances of a sacred nature on the mountain north of their city. However they immediately laid plans for the building of temples.

As a boy I used to go to the temple block and watch the brethren cutting the great granite stones—each one numbered and cut to measure, so that it would fit in the exact spot for which it was intended. I can still hear the contact of the chisel upon the stone.

Lord Commands Saints to Build Temple

When the Latter-day Saints became settled in a body in Kirtland, one of the first commandments the Lord gave to them was to build a temple. Therefore in their poverty, but with faith, they went to work and built the Kirtland Temple.

My grandfather Hyrum Smith and Reynolds Cahoon commenced the digging of the trench for the foundation of the Kirtland Temple on the fifth day of June 1833. All of the brethren went to work with their might, for they realized the necessity of a sacred house built to the name of the Lord. The most important reason for the building of the Kirtland Temple was that there might be a sacred place dedicated to the name of the Lord to which his ancient servants might come, as the Savior did himself, to restore the covenants and authorities of the Holy Priesthood. It was in that temple that the Savior appeared, and angels were seen by many at the time of the dedication.

First of all came the Savior who accepted the house, and the temple was filled with the glory of the Lord. It was in that temple that Moses came, committing the keys of the gathering of Israel. Elias who lived in the days of Abraham, committed the keys of the dispensation of Abraham; and Elijah came, fulfilling the promise of the Lord through Malachi, turning the hearts of the fathers to the children and the children to their fathers. The evidence of this fulfilment is apparent, for from that day the hearts of thousands of children have turned to their dead fathers, and the great work of research and preparation of the records of the dead has taken hold of the children who are today working in genealogical research, preparing the way for the performance of temple work for the dead.

38

The Identity of Elijah and Elias

Question: *"Who is Elias referred to in Section 110 of the Doctrine and Covenants? It appears that the Elias who visited the apostles on the Mount of Transfiguration was Elijah, but both Elias and Elijah appeared to the Prophet Joseph Smith and Oliver Cowdery in the Kirtland Temple."*

Answer: So many questions have been received from those who seem to be in a quandary concerning the identity of Elijah and Elias spoken of in the revelation in the Doctrine and Covenants, Section 110, and also in the Bible,[1] that the following explanation has been prepared.

Elijah.—A prophet of Israel, from Gilead, east of the Jordan. He was known as Elijah the Tishbite and lived in the days of Ahab, one of the most wicked kings of Israel. Elijah was one of the greatest of the prophets, and the Lord conferred upon him the sealing power. The Prophet Joseph Smith has said that Elijah was the last of the prophets in old Israel, that is before the coming of our Savior, who held the fulness of divine authority. He had power to seal and bind, and did exercise authority over the elements as well as over the destinies of man. Holding these important keys of the binding and

---

[1]Matthew, Chapter 17.

sealing power, the Lord appointed him to come in the last days and restore his authority upon Joseph Smith and Oliver Cowdery, thus fulfilling the prediction made by Malachi. In the Greek language he is referred to as Elias and in the Catholic edition of the Bible he is referred to as Elias all through the Old Testament as well as in the New. In the New Testament, it having come to us from the Greek, he is given the name of Elias.

Elias.—A name given to the prophet who held the keys of the dispensation in which Abraham lived, spoken of in Section 110 of the Doctrine and Covenants. The scriptures do not reveal to us who this prophet really was, but the Prophet Joseph Smith declared that he was Noah,[2] who is spoken of as Elias in the Doctrine and Covenants, Section 27:7.

Elias Is also a Title

This name (Elias) is a *title* which is applied to several prophets, and has reference to their *office* as messengers sent to prepare the way for a greater work. John the Baptist is spoken of as Elias, because he prepared the way before the ministry of the Lord. Joseph Smith is an Elias because he was sent to prepare the way for the second coming of our Lord.

The Prophet has explained in his teachings the differences in the missions of Elias, Elijah, and Messiah.

> The spirit of Elias is first, Elijah second, and Messiah last. Elias is a forerunner to prepare the way, and the spirit and power of Elijah is to come after, holding the keys of power, building the Temple to the capstone, placing the seals of the Melchizedek

---

[2]See "Elias Is Noah," *Answers to Gospel Questions*, Vol. 3, pp. 138-141.

Priesthood upon the house of Israel, and making all things ready; then Messiah comes to His Temple, which is last of all.

Messiah is above the spirit and power of Elijah, for He made the world, and was that spiritual rock unto Moses in the wilderness. . . .[3]

---

[3]*Teachings of the Prophet Joseph Smith,* p. 340. Read also pp. 172, 323, 335-341.

39

The Importance of Temple Marriage

Question: *"What does a young woman or a young man do who marries outside of the temple of the Lord?"*[1]

Answer: Unless young people who marry outside the temple speedily repent, they cut themselves off from exaltation in the celestial kingdom of God. If they should prove themselves worthy, notwithstanding that great error, to enter into the celestial kingdom, they go in that kingdom as servants.

What does that mean? The revelation tells us they go into that kingdom to be servants to those who are worthy of a more highly exalted position—something with greater glory. They are servants to them. They don't become sons and daughters of God. They are not joint heirs with Jesus Christ. They do not obtain the kingdom, that is, the crown and the glory of the kingdom of God. They who are married in the temple for time and eternity, if they are true and faithful to their covenants, enter into that kingdom. They are heirs of that kingdom, joint heirs with Jesus Christ, sons and daughters of God, entitled to the fulness of the kingdom.

---

[1]Answer given to question at afternoon session of Ensign Stake Conference, Assembly Hall, October 31, 1954, as reported by Lola E. Meehan.

Have No Claim upon Each Other

When they marry outside of the temple, they cut themselves off. If they are content with that kind of marriage outside, when they come forth in the resurrection, they have no claim upon each other, or their children upon them, and there will be weeping, wailing and gnashing of teeth.

Those who are married in the temple for all time and eternity obtain the blessing of *eternal lives.* I put stress on *eternal lives.* Eternal life is God's life, that is, to be like him. *Eternal lives* means eternal increase—the continuation, as the revelation says, of the seeds forever. To be married outside of the temple is for time only. Death separates—that is an eternal separation, unless in the meantime they repent and are fortunate enough to go to the temple and make amends.

Children born to them under the covenant—that is, to parents married in the temple—are entitled to blessings which children outside of the covenant are not entitled to receive. The Lord speaks of marriage outside of the temple as "entering into the deaths—eternal deaths." That doesn't mean they are going to die again. Every soul will get the resurrection. But after the resurrection comes the segregation into kingdoms—celestial, terrestrial, telestial, and then to be cast out—which will come to some—with the devil and his angels. Where they go, I don't know. The Lord has spoken of it as outer darkness. So the Lord prepares places for all. *Eternal deaths* means that they are separately and singly forever. They have no increase. The Lord calls that death. They do not continue—that is, they do not continue through posterity—they come to an end.

Individuals Make Own Choice

Now, if our young people choose that sort of life, if that's what they want, I leave it for them. My father on many occasions gathered his children together and instructed them. He said he would rather take them to the grave and lay them away in their purity because they would be entitled to the blessings of the kingdom of God, than to see them marry outside of the house of the Lord—unless they repented—or to marry outside of the Church. Some of our parents don't seem to care.

I pick up the evening newspaper sometimes, and I see pictures of very beautiful girls—they don't put the pictures of the handsome boys in the papers—and I discover that those girls—many of them are daughters of parents who are married in the temple and the children were born under the covenant—marry outside of the temple, maybe outside of the Church. . . .

But these parents see to it that the picture is put in the paper, with a fine article telling how the daughter is going to be dressed, whom she is marrying, what kind of reception they are going to have, and they seem to be very happy. They should put on sackcloth and sit in ashes. What are they doing? Of course there is such a thing as repentance. They should pray for that repentance. But they should weep, not rejoice; they should be sorry, not pleased, for they are assisting—if they have never taught their children better—they are assisting in sending those children to the deaths eternally.

Where Does the Blame Lie?

Now, did you ever think of this? This is the condition we find in every stake of Zion. Where does the blame lie? Well, it may be a little with all of us, with the teachers who visit the home, with those who talk to the members of the Church in sacrament meetings, the bishops of wards, all who hold the priesthood; but primarily it rests upon the shoulders of the parents for not teaching those children from their infancy, beginning to instruct them as soon as they can understand, what the kingdom of God means, what exaltation in it means, and how it can be obtained.

I tell you, I would weep if I had a child who would marry outside of the temple of the Lord. Fortunately I never had such a thing happen. I am grateful for that. My children have married good companions—all of them active in the Church, all of them happy in their membership. What will happen to the next generation, I don't know. But my children were taught and I am grateful that they have followed the advice of their parents.

Now, if you are at fault, my good brothers and sisters, go to the Lord on your knees and ask for forgiveness and see if you can't amend the evil, repair the broken commandment for which you no doubt are partly, at least, responsible. If you have done all of those—taught your children the best you could and they rebel against you—of course you go before the Lord and tell him that your hands are clean, the children are rebellious. People do have rebellious children. Adam had rebellious children. Evidently the greater part of his family were rebellious. People have an idea that Adam had only three sons, but our Doctrine and Covenants and Pearl of Great Price tell us differently. He lived a long time —had children for many, many years, had children for hundreds of years until they became numerous upon the face of the earth. And although I am sure he tried to teach them, many of them rebelled. That can't always be avoided, but it can quite generally be avoided if the parents are doing their duty, if they are living as they should live, keeping the commandments of the Lord, being true and faithful to every covenant they make.

The Problem of Divorce

I would like to say much about divorce. When you go home, you pick up your Bible and turn to the nineteenth chapter of Matthew, read the first nine verses. I get letters sometimes from people who say, "What are we going to do? In Matthew it reads so and so and yet the Church is not following it strictly." Well, I write back and say I have no authority to change the word of the Lord. Read it. There are too many divorces in this Church, too many separations—many of them without proper cause. And I have said before, and I am going to repeat it: There never will be a divorce among those married in the temple if both of the parties, husband and wife, are living their religion; they will never separate. How can they if they keep the commandments of the Lord?

I read this morning to you from the fourth book of Nephi how they were given in marriage and how happy they were, raising large families, multiplying, blessed by the Spirit of the Lord. They didn't have any separations. They were not torn asunder because there wasn't any wickedness among them. That is the way we ought to live.

40

Why Take the Gospel to Asia?

Question: *"Why take the gospel to Asia? Is there any of the blood of Israel in those Oriental countries?"*[1]

Answer: My dear brothers and sisters, and that includes all of you, I was very grateful to go to the Orient and while there [in 1955] to dedicate Korea and the Philippines, Japan having already been dedicated. It was a great opportunity to have this privilege of meeting with some of those good people over there. I found faithful members of the Church in Korea. If time permitted I would tell you a story in regard to one young man that I ordained to the office of a deacon. How grateful he was. A boy, maybe fourteen years of age! He lived up on the hillside in the city of Seoul, among people who were poor, almost, it seemed to me, destitute. I never felt more sorry for anybody in all my life than I did for those people over there. But this young man was so grateful to hold the priesthood. . . .

I had a very enjoyable visit among the people of Korea when I was there.

A Question Frequently Asked

Now I have been asked the question a score of times

---

[1]Address delivered at the "Spotlight on Asia" banquet at Brigham Young University, November 15, 1962.

since I returned if I thought there was any of the blood of Israel in those Oriental countries. And some of the people who ask me that question, ask it with sort of a feeling, it seemed to me, that the blood of Israel just could not have penetrated there.

I am going to take a little time on that, by reading the blessing of Abraham.

> Now the Lord had said unto Abram, Get thee out of thy country, and from thy kindred, and from thy father's house, unto a land that I will shew thee:
>
> And I will make of thee a great nation, and I will bless thee and make thy name great; and thou shalt be a blessing:
>
> And I will bless them that bless thee, and curse him that curseth thee; and in thee shall all families of the earth be blessed.[2]

Now there's the answer. I turn over to the twenty-second chapter. I want to read you three verses.

> And the angel of the Lord called unto Abraham out of heaven the second time,
>
> And said, By myself have I sworn, saith the Lord, for because thou hast done this thing, and hast not withheld thy son, thine only son:

[I will pause in the middle of the sentence. You know what it was, it was the willingness on the part of Abraham to offer his son Isaac on the altar. Now I'll continue the quotation.]

> That in blessing I will bless thee, and in multiplying I will multiply thy seed as the stars of the heaven, and as the sand which is upon the sea shore; and thy seed shall possess the gate of his enemies;

---

[2]Genesis 12:1-3.

And in thy seed shall all the nations of the earth be blessed; because thou hast obeyed my voice.[3]

Now I think that is a sufficient answer to those people who think that the people of the Orient are not entitled to receive the gospel of Jesus Christ.

Book of Mormon Evidence on Subject

But we have something in the Book of Mormon that, if we did not have any other truth expressed in it, would be sufficient evidence of the divinity of this book. I have reference to the fifth chapter of Jacob. In this chapter we have a parable that nobody could have written unless he had the guidance of the Spirit of the Lord. It would have been impossible. I think that as many as ninety-nine out of every hundred who read the Book of Mormon, read this parable through without grasping the fulness and meaning of it. And I think this is one of the greatest passages in the Book of Mormon. If I had time I would read all of it to you. But I am going to ask you, no matter how many times you have read the Book of Mormon, to take a few minutes at some convenient time and sit down and just read carefully every word in the fifth chapter of the Book of Jacob. It is a parable. No greater parable was ever recorded. It is a parable of the scattering of Israel. The Lord revealed to Jacob that he would scatter Israel, and in this figure, Israel is a tame olive tree. It is an olive tree that begins to decay. The branches that are dying are cut off. But the gardener takes certain of those branches off that tree that seem to be decaying and plants them in all parts of the Lord's vineyard. And the Lord says,

---

[3]*Ibid.*, 22:15-18.

"I will take these branches and plant them in the distant parts of my vineyard. Have my servants attend to them. The old tree seems to be dying and we shall see if we can't take these severed branches and raise fruit."

Not only that, but they took some of the branches and grafted them in to all the wild olive trees. Who were the wild olive trees? The Gentiles. And so the Lord sent his servants to all parts of his vineyard, which is the world, and planted these branches of the tree. As they grew, they bore fruit. In the course of time, some of these branches began to wither and decay. And the Lord nurtured them. He had his servants dig around them, cultivate them, care for them the best they knew how, and yet some of them practically died. Others bore fruit. Then comes the time of the harvest. The Lord says, "I will cultivate my field for the last time. These branches that I have taken to various parts of the world are dying. I'll gather the fruit and do the best I can with them."

The Olive Tree Is the House of Israel

Now that in substance is the revelation given to Jacob. There is not a greater parable in the Bible or anywhere else, and yet we read it through and fail to grasp the meaning of it.

Now in that parable the olive tree is the House of Israel, as I have said. In its native land it began to die. So the Lord took branches like the Nephites, like the lost tribes, and like others that the Lord led off that we do not know anything about, to other parts of the earth. He planted them all over his vineyard, which is the world. No doubt he sent some of these branches into

Japan, into Korea, into China. No question about it, because he sent them to all parts of the world.

Time came when in these distant parts the trees began to decay, so the Lord sent out for the last time to gather the fruit into the harvest.

Let me read just a few last verses.

And it came to pass that the Lord of the vineyard said unto the servant: Let us go to and hew down the trees of the vineyard and cast them into the fire, that they shall not cumber the ground of my vineyard, for I have done all. What could I have done more for my vineyard?

But, behold, the servant said unto the Lord of the vineyard: Spare it a little longer.

And the Lord said: Yea, I will spare it a little longer, for it grieveth me that I should lose the trees of my vineyard.

Wherefore, let us take of the branches of these which I have planted in the nethermost parts of my vineyard, and let us graft them into the tree from whence they came; and let us pluck from the tree those branches whose fruit is most bitter, and graft in the natural branches of the tree in the stead thereof.

And this will I do that the tree may not perish, that, perhaps I may preserve unto myself the roots thereof for mine own purpose.

And, behold, the roots of the natural branches of the tree which I planted whithersoever I would are yet alive; wherefore, that I may preserve them also for mine own purpose, I will take of the branches of this tree, and I will graft them in unto them. Yea, I will graft in unto them the branches of their mother tree, that I may preserve the roots also unto mine own self. . . .[4]

Now we get to the finish.

For behold, for a long time will I lay up of the fruit of

[4]Jacob 5:49-54.

my vineyard unto mine own self against the season, which speedily cometh; and for the last time have I nourished the vineyard, and pruned it, and dug about it, and dunged it; wherefore I will lay up unto mine own self of the fruit, for a long time, according to that which I have spoken.

And when the time cometh that evil fruit shall again come into my vineyard,

[Now that doesn't sound too good because that means there will be some apostasy.]

. . . then will I cause the good and the bad to be gathered; and the good will I preserve unto myself, and the bad will I cast away into its own place. And then cometh the season and the end; and my vineyard will I cause to be burned with fire.[5]

Written by the Inspiration of the Almighty

When you go home, read that chapter through. I tell you, my brothers and sisters, Joseph Smith did not write it. That was written by the inspiration of the Almighty.

Now there is your answer. That is the answer to these people who approach me with the question, what's the use of going out among the Chinese, the Japanese, the Koreans, and the people of the Far East to preach the gospel to them? The answer: because they are branches of the tree, they are of the house of Israel. The Lord took the branches of the tree, grafted them into the wild olives, the Gentiles, and is bringing the Gentiles into the gospel of Jesus Christ.

When you read that chapter through if you cannot say in your soul, "This is absolutely a revelation from

[5]*Ibid.*, 5:76-77.

God," then there is something wrong with you. That tells you of history. Are we going to preach the gospel in Korea, in Japan, in China? Yes, we are. Why? Because the blood of Israel is there. And the Lord did just what he said he would do with Abraham and his posterity. He scattered them over the whole face of the earth. So now the Gentiles are sanctified by the blood of Abraham.

41

Temporal Laws of the Gospel

Question: *"Are we placing too much stress on temporal laws of the gospel?"*[1]

Answer: Brigham Young once said, "In the mind of God there is no such a thing as dividing spiritual from temporal, or temporal from spiritual; for they are one in the Lord."[2]

The Lord has given us certain laws and ordinances that pertain to our salvation. We make some of them temporal laws. For instance, we may look upon the keeping of the Sabbath day holy largely as a temporal law. When you read what the Lord said, that everything should rest—even the cattle, the teams of horses or oxen or whatever they had should have a day of rest as well as man—we might get the idea that this is a temporal law.

The Lord says in Section 29 of the Doctrine and Covenants that at no time has he given a temporal law.

> Wherefore, verily I say unto you that all things unto me are spiritual, and not at any time have I given unto you a law which was temporal; neither any man, nor the children of men; neither Adam, your father, whom I created.[3]

---

[1]Answer to this question was reported in a sermon delivered in the Salt Lake Eighteenth Ward, August 9, 1959.

[2]*Discourses of Brigham Young*, p. 20.

[3]D. & C. 29:34.

Now he gave instruction to the brethren in early days more than he has in more recent times on how to build houses. The Lord told them what the dimensions should be. He gave them instructions about building other things, about the people looking after their farms, cattle, etc., by revelation, whether they were to build a fence or printing plant or anything else. Everything the Lord has commanded his people to do has a bearing upon our spiritual and eternal salvation.

The Lord's Words Have Spiritual Background

The Lord frequently has given instructions that to many with our mortal minds would appear to be of a temporal character; but nevertheless, everything that he has done for the benefit of man has a spiritual background to it. The keeping of the Sabbath day holy, the building of the Nauvoo House—which was nothing more or less than a hotel which was to take care of strangers—whatever it has been, it has been for the spiritual salvation of the members of the Church.

The Lord gave instructions with regard to schools where our people, both old and young, could go and be educated. Well, those are the temporal commandments. They were commandments to help the people, to prepare them for eternity and everything the Lord has commanded.

In the laying out of cities—now the Lord gave a plan for a city to the Prophet Joseph Smith. It would have been a perfect city. Salt Lake City was laid out in the beginning according to that plan—four-square, ten-acre blocks, wide streets. That's the way the city was to be built. They used to make fun of the Latter-day Saints, Brigham Young in particular, because we had such wide streets. They were too wide. Now in the days of automobiles they don't think they are wide enough. And so some foolish fellows are cutting wider streets for us, destroying property, making it inconvenient for people in order to make wider streets in some places. These modern planners who build have built into this city in such a way that you can't tell where they live according to the number of their homes. They have twisted streets, turned them, built them on angles, made dead ends to some of them and everything else. You ride out in that section of the county, it looks beautiful, but I want to tell you, Brothers and Sisters, the Lord did not have a hand in the building of them—twisting and turning and making alleys, crowded streets with dead ends. That's the way they build in the world.

The Lord Inspired the Prophet Joseph Smith

Now I could say a lot about what is in my mind about criticizing those who think they know so much, but that would be all out of order. We come here to worship the Lord, don't we, and keep his commandments? Well, I want to tell you that the Lord inspired the Prophet Joseph Smith when he gave him the plan for the City of Zion. When President Brigham Young and the pioneers came here they followed that instruction. Modern men without inspiration don't have that same spirit.

What does the Sabbath day mean to many of the members of the Church? I don't know, but I suppose there is a baseball game going on tonight—maybe in our city. No doubt there will be thousands of people there if there is being one played. Thousands of people shouting, calling to members of the teams to do this and that and so-forth, entering into a lot of confusion. It is the Sabbath day. If no members of the Church would go to that ball park on the Sabbath day, they would not play there. It would not pay them. The Gentile population would not, in my opinion, be sufficient to support the team on the Sabbath, and there are some people who don't belong to the Church who are as sincere in keeping the Sabbath day as members of the Church—those who do keep it. . . .

Keep the commandments, though temporal or spiritual they may seem. They all have a spiritual purpose.

42

Is There a Contradiction between Jacob 2:24-27 and D. & C. 132:39?

Question: *"Representatives of the Jehovah's Witnesses called at my home and endeavored to disprove statements in the Book of Mormon. Among other things they claimed there was a discrepancy between Jacob 2:24-27 and Doctrine and Covenants 132:39. It was also their contention that the doctrine of plural marriage was condemned in the Book of Jacob and that the practice of this principle in the early days of the Church was not only a contradiction of Bible doctrine but also of the Book of Mormon. Will you please give answer to this problem?*

Answer: As far as the Book of Mormon is concerned, it requires no defense from me nor anyone else. Moroni has given a challenge to the world in Moroni 10:3-5. Many thousands have accepted it and have proved the Book of Mormon true. This can be proved by anyone else if he will follow Moroni's teachings. I cannot take the time to go into detail about the testimonies of the witnesses.[1] It is enough for me to say that under all circumstances *not one* of these wit-

---

[1]The Divine Law of Witnesses is explained in detail in *Answers to Gospel Questions*, Vol. 1, pp. 202-207, and *Doctrines of Salvation*, Vol. 1, pp. 203-228. See especially pp. 222-228 of the latter volume for a discussion of the testimony of the three witnesses to the Book of Mormon.

nesses ever denied his testimony. I have a letter written by Oliver Cowdery in his own handwriting in which he bears testimony, and this only a short time before his death.

The verses in question are as follows:

> Behold, David and Solomon truly had many wives and concubines, which thing was abominable before me, saith the Lord.
>
> Wherefore, thus saith the Lord, I have led this people forth out of the land of Jerusalem, by the power of mine arm, that I might raise up unto me a righteous branch from the fruit of the loins of Joseph.
>
> Wherefore, I the Lord God will not suffer that this people shall do like unto them of old.
>
> Wherefore, my brethren, hear me, and hearken to the word of the Lord: For there shall not any man among you have save it be one wife; and concubines he shall have none;[2]

And from the Doctrine and Covenants:

> David's wives and concubines were given unto him of me, by the hand of Nathan, my servant, and others of the prophets who had the keys of this power; and in none of these things did he sin against me save in the case of Uriah and his wife; and, therefore he hath fallen from his exaltation, and received his portion; and he shall not inherit them out of the world, for I gave them unto another, saith the Lord.[3]

THERE IS NO CONTRADICTION

There is no contradiction between Jacob and the Doctrine and Covenants. Jacob, in the Book of Mormon,

---

[2]Jacob 2:24-27.
[3]D. & C. 132:39.

declared that the Lord prevented the Nephites from practicing plural marriage and called attention to the fact that David and Solomon sinned in taking wives that the Lord did not give them, which is true. However, the key to the situation may be found by reading further the account in Jacob. The Lord said:

> For if I will, saith the Lord of Hosts, raise up seed unto me, I will command my people; otherwise they shall hearken unto these things.[4]

Is it not strange that the Lord did not condemn Abraham and Jacob (Israel) upon whom he founded the House of Israel; nor did he condemn the parents of Samuel, the great prophet, nor others who had plural wives; nor did he condemn others who had plural families. He did not condemn Solomon and David for having wives *which the Lord gave them.*

Now turn to II Samuel, 12:7-8, and you will find that the Lord gave David wives. In your reading of the Old Testament you will also find that Solomon was blessed and the Lord appeared to him and gave him visions and great blessings when he had plural wives, but later in his life, he took wives that the Lord did not give him. For evidence of this, turn to I Kings 11, and read it. You can tell these people that the whole house of Israel was built on the twelve sons of Jacob who had four wives—mothers of the House of Israel.

History of a Man-made Religion

Now it would be well for you to study the background of the Jehovah's Witnesses, and find out what a

---

[4]Jacob 2:30.

shaky foundation they are standing on. I have followed them for many years. This organization was founded by Charles Taze Russell of Allegheny, Pittsburgh in 1872. He was a member of the Congregational Church. This organization is not one revealed from heaven. Russell left the Congregational Church and started an organization which was called Zion's Watchtower Society, then International Bible Students, and now they have presumed to call themselves Jehovah's Witnesses. They have had no revelation from heaven, and claim none, but have assumed to call themselves by this name. It seems that their main purpose is to attack The Church of Jesus Christ of Latter-day Saints. Many years ago their battle cry was that "there are millions now living who will never die." For some reason we do not hear this now. It is one of the man-made religions by dissatisfied members of other Christian churches.

If they had the spirit of sincerity they would not be going around bearing false witness of others and putting forth dishonest statements and quoting from disreputable publications about The Church of Jesus Christ of Latter-day Saints.

APPENDIX

Questions answered in volumes I, II, and III:

INDEX

—C—

—D—

—F—

—G—